Battle Tested

Breaking Through Challenges to Live Your Best Life Now

by

Dr. Paula Olivier

Watersprings
PUBLISHING

Published by Watersprings Publishing, a division of
Watersprings Media House, LLC.
P.O. Box 1284
Olive Branch, MS 38654
www.waterspringsmedia.com
Contact publisher for bulk orders and permission requests.

Printed in the United States of America.

Library of Congress Control Number: 2020906316

ISBN-13: 978-1-948877-56-5

Dedication

To my loving husband Smith Olivier, D.Min, PhD
and to my parents Eugenie and Daniel Fils-Aimé, Sr.

Acknowledgments

To my best friend Dr. Kyna Griffith-Henry, Mrs. Frederica Griffith, Dr. Carveson Griffith, Bishop Millicent Hunter, Bishop Rosie O'Neal, Dr. Kim Logan Nowlan-thank you for taking the time to review my work and for providing valuable feedback. I am also grateful to Pastor Samuel G. Campbell for what he taught me about church administration. I am especially indebted to Dr. Frederick Russell for believing in me and giving me my start in ministry.

Table of Contents

Introduction

It had been four months since I'd had to interact with people. When you get a cancer diagnosis like I did, sometimes there is a series of surgeries that follow. For this particular surgery I had in February 2013, it would take me four months to recover. I had to take time off work. I could not entertain guests in my home.

My husband was my primary caretaker. When he was away at work, I was home alone. I had so much time on my hands, spring cleaning came early. I cleaned every corner of the house. If I wasn't cleaning, I was reading. I consumed books about my two passions—the Bible and leadership. The books increased my academic knowledge, but because of the extended absence of people, my social skills began to suffer. That can be a career-killer for a pastor.

Fast forward four months: approximately 120 days after surgery, I went back to work. I walked through the church doors, and members and friends were ecstatic! Hugs, kisses, cheers, handshakes, greetings—I know that sounds exciting. But the truth is, returning to work was like coming out of solitary confinement. So, EVERY interaction sent me into sensory overload. All the hugs, kisses, greetings, and conversations were nice, but they required a level of mental processing I hadn't had to engage for months. Part of me wanted to place my hands over my ears, retreat into a corner, sit in silence, and collect myself. But I couldn't do that. They wouldn't understand. So instead, I stood there. I spoke. I greeted. I laughed. But inside I wanted to run away.

This was not the first forced hiatus I had to take from work. But it was related to the same diagnosis. This second time around felt like, "Here we go again." Have you ever felt that way? Here we go again! Standing still when you feel like running, conversing when you'd rather be silent, interacting when you want to be left alone? I was leading, chairing meetings, preaching, counseling, problem solving, while everything inside me wanted to scream "Stop!" and call it quits. That was my daily inward struggle.

This went on for weeks. To get through it, no matter what was going through my mind, I had to act normal until I felt normal. When you go through a crisis, you quickly learn what people around you are slow to grasp: "Normal" takes time. People like to say, "She made a comeback." Let me tell you something, when life knocks you down, you don't just come back. You battle back.

My experiences have taught me in order to do life well, it helps to be battle-tested. As a matter of fact, negative experiences are an inevitable part of our existence and are incredibly formative. Fortunately, they do not always result in the emergence of flaws or setbacks later in life, they can also precipitate the development of positive traits. For instance, a person may embrace certain attributes as a way of preventing the formation of a particular flaw. Someone who was abused may choose to develop patience, kindness, and tolerance. Overcoming sickness can teach one how imperative it is to live fully and the importance of being in the moment. What is more, the qualities needed to overcome adversity correspond with those needed to achieve success, such as building resolve, thriving in various troubling situations, and remaining poised under pressure.

Life is indeed hard, but it's not impossible. There will be challenges, but there are also strategies one can utilize to navigate difficulties detailed in the chapters ahead. In this book, I report some lighthearted moments as well as some serious ones. Most of all, I try to share a few lessons to help you succeed from my battle-tested life.

Battle Lessons from the Storm

There are no great people in this world,
only great challenges which ordinary people rise to meet.

-William Frederick Halsey, Jr.

CHAPTER 1

The desire to make progress is fundamental to human nature. We see it in our traditions of celebrating milestones such as birthdays, graduations, anniversaries, victories, and promotions. Think of the cakes, birthday candles, balloons, restaurant dinners, friends who traveled across long distances to come celebrate the honoree. Those are fond memories. We all want to make progress in life, but some seem to do it just a bit better. If we're honest, there are those who do it a whole lot better than others. What is their secret? How do they do it? Research reveals there's not one specific practice that produces great success. It's a combination of a few factors. One chief factor is disposition.

We may not say it out loud, but many people silently believe life should be easy. This quiet conviction shows when we run into difficulties. When we encounter problems, we are quick to protest that life is so unfair. When we aren't succeeding, we feel like somebody played dirty, the deck is stacked against us, or we got a raw deal. The bitter feelings that come with that pattern of thinking can dampen our drive and kill our momentum.

Business Insider and Inc. magazine identified John Maxwell as the most influential leadership expert in the world. He's also a New York Times bestselling author. Maxwell wrote, "Because we want to believe life should be easy, we sometimes assume anything that's difficult must be impossible."[1] That's a powerful statement. This silent assumption puts us at odds with achieving our goals. It can lead us to criticize whatever seems impossible, unattainable, or even challenging. We say things like, "Who wants that promotion anyway? It's just a lot more responsibility and headache." Those rationalizations seem harmless at first. However, they have a way of catching up with us. After a while, we look around and realize we're in the same place, doing the same thing, answering to the same people. We wonder why we feel stuck, underappreciated, and dissatisfied. It's because we are trying to dodge difficulty. Sometimes it's because we feel overwhelmed.

Anxiety happens when you think you have to figure out everything all at once. Breathe. You're strong. You got this. Take it day by day.

-Karen Salmansohn

The most influential person in my spiritual life taught me how to confront whatever is confronting you. She's five feet two inches tall with a quiet demeanor. You wouldn't think it to look at her, but this woman has exerted more influence on those around her than you can imagine. Who is she? She's my mother. What has she done? Pay close attention.

My mom used to be the secretary of our family business. However, her passion is unquestionably church planting. Anyone who has ever tried to plant a church can testify that it is one of the most draining, time-consuming, self-sacrificing endeavors to take on. She doesn't get paid to do it, but she is currently planting her third church. How does she do it? How does this natural introvert rally the support she needs to make the impossible probable and the probable possible?

August 24, 1992, Hurricane Andrew ravaged through my hometown in Miami, Florida. I was a teenager at the time. We hunkered down in the room that had the least number of windows. Fear kept me in my father's arms—sheltering us from the madness of the storm. We heard the most horrible sounds of objects—sharp, blunt, large, and small—crashing through every window in the house except the room where we huddled for safety. Water from the coast invaded our room and flooded the ground. After several hours of wondering whether we would live or die, Hurricane Andrew finally passed. When daylight came, we all walked outside and saw what looked like a war zone. The interiors of many houses were laid open to the naked eye. Roofs caved in. Towering trees had been uprooted and laid on their sides. Cars were overturned. It was a pitiful sight. Some wept, some cried, many people died.

Fortunately, my mother had weathered the storm in a nearby hospital. She had taken my grandparents there for safety. When she came home, she witnessed the devastation to our home. The mailbox had taken flight during the storm. We had no idea where it was. The front windows were shattered. The neighbor's car rolled over the fence and was lying wheels up in our front yard. The good news is we still had a roof. The bad news is, our backyard looked like a fallen jungle.

When we bought the house, the fence in the backyard was already lined with trees. My mother had taken it upon herself also to plant an orange tree, an avocado tree, passion fruit, sugar cane, and a mango tree (Did I mention that my mom also loves to plant?). Consequently, when the storm came, it toppled everything. You could hardly make your way through the entire yard. Everyone knew it was going to take a lot of work to clear the yard, and none of us were looking forward to the task.

The next morning, my father went to North Miami to check on the office and to purchase us food. My mother got up, walked around the house waking everybody up. "Come on. Let's go!

We have to clean the yard." At the sound of those words, my siblings and I feigned extreme fatigue. No one budged because no one wanted to touch the yard. After a while, we heard silence. My mother stopped calling our names. We all thought we had succeeded in fooling my mother into thinking we were all still sleeping. Alas, the yard work would have to wait for another day. So we thought.

I will never forget what happened next. Soon, we all heard a strange sound, "kling, kling, kling." Slowly, we rose from our beds to find the source of this mysterious noise. Looking out of the window, we finally found it. There she was, my mother—the five-foot two-inch introvert— with machete in hand, hammering away at one of the fallen trees. The tree was twice her size, but it didn't seem to matter to her. Alone and surrounded with what seemed like an impossible task, my mother was hammering away.

We were shocked and in awe at the same time. Without uttering much, my siblings and I rose to our feet, washed up, and joined my mother outside. We took up the remaining gardening tools the storm had left us. We asked my mom for the machete and sent her inside to relax. Then my four siblings and I began chopping, cleaning, dragging, and gathering. By the time it was nightfall, we had cleared most of the yard. Because of my mother's wisdom, the task that once seemed impossible was now nearly completed. What a shot in the arm! If they needed it, we were ready to take on our neighbors' yards.

What did I learn from my mother's actions? Audacity is contagious. When you step up to the plate to face your challenges, those on the sidelines begin to see life through your eyes. They take a brief mental break from their self-imposed limitations and begin to believe.

We did not want to get out of bed because all we saw awaiting us was chaos. But our mom's action gave us the courage to take a second look. You see, chaos is unmanageable, but fallen trees can be moved. Trunks can be cut. Twigs can be gathered. Debris can be assembled and put away. It turned out we were more than able to accomplish our assignment.

Could the same be true for you? Are you facing a difficult course in school? Tutors can be reached. Libraries can be frequented. Studies can be augmented. Are you overwhelmed by a fractured relationship? Pride can be swallowed. Forgiveness can be offered. Apologies can be made. Are you worried about finding a decent job? Degrees can be earned—skills can be learned, and networks can be established.

The old riddle asks, "How do you eat an elephant?" The answer is simple, "One bite at a time." The next time you feel overwhelmed by the challenge in front of you, remember the sound of a machete striking against a fallen tree. Picture five inspired teens taking on the wreckage of a mighty storm. Give your task a second look. You are more than able to conquer your assignment.

Application Exercises

1. Who have been the two most influential people in your life and why?

_____

_____

_____

_____

_____

2. Select a challenge you are currently facing. How would you break down the challenge into smaller, achievable steps?

_____

_____

_____

_____

_____

3. There are so many things that require your attention. Prioritize your tasks for the day. Which should you complete first, second, third, etc.?

_____

_____

_____

_____

_____

Battle Lessons
from the Aftermath

Being challenged in life is inevitable,
being defeated is optional.

-Roger Crawford

CHAPTER 2

I have learned that you can escape the brunt of a storm only to be caught by its aftermath. It took years for the neighborhood to recover from Hurricane Andrew. Sometime after the storm, my mother took me to check on one of the properties we owned. She was speaking with the neighbor in the front yard while I went to check on something in the backyard. I don't remember what I was looking for.

But whatever it was, I got more than I bargained for.

It was my senior year in high school, and my guidance counselor entered me in an oratorical contest. The winner would receive a two- year full scholarship to Miami-Dade Community College (MDCC). If I won, the plan was to attend MDCC and complete my bachelor's degree at Florida International University. My plans began to unravel the very day of that property visit.

The competition was that evening at 8:00pm. My mom and I stopped by the cleaners earlier to pick up my outfit for the competition. It was a peach dress with a white satin bow on the side. The dress was now in the car. While in the backyard, I heard my mom call out to me that we were leaving. As I was racing from the back of the house, I leaped into the air to jump over some pieces of plywood on the ground. I cleared one, but not the other. I didn't know anything was wrong until I tried to lift my right foot. It did not move. I pulled, and it still would not budge. Then I grabbed my right ankle with both hands and lifted my foot upward. I saw why I had trouble moving it. I stepped on a large, rusty nail. It had penetrated my sneakers. As I continued walking to the front yard, I began to feel something warm and wet in my shoe. I went to the car, removed the sneaker, and saw that my sock was soaked in blood. When my mom saw the blood, she immediately rushed me to the emergency clinic.

The competition was in a few hours. Everyone knows it takes forever to be seen in the emergency room. My mom sat in the waiting room with me. We were both silent. We knew the scholarship was slipping away. I began to offer a silent prayer to God. "Lord, please, you know how important this is to me. If I get this scholarship, my parents won't have to pay for school. Please, God, help me get out of here."

About an hour before the competition, I was treated and released. It was a miracle! I was excited! I told my mom, "Let's go straight to MDCC campus for the competition." My mom looked at me and said, "You can't go dressed like that." I know I was wearing blue jeans and a T-shirt, but considering the circumstances, it's better to show up casual than to miss the entire competition. I begged. I pleaded, but my mom wouldn't hear any of it. She took me home to change.

I put on my peach dress with the white satin bow on the side. She made me put on stockings--yes, stockings over my injured and heavily bandaged foot. I forced my foot into a pair of white pumps and limped to the car. I was nervously reviewing my speech on the way. By the time we reached the campus, the competition had already begun. My mom dropped me off while she went to look for parking. I was limping around the campus, asking passersby after passersby for directions to the proper building. I was pointed to the elevator.

On my way up to the second floor, I prayed and prayed hard. When the elevator doors opened, I saw my guidance counselor standing in front of me. He threw his hands in the air and said, "There you are!" I tried to explain what happened. "I'm sorry. I had an emergency. My foot was bleeding..." He said, "Follow me." He rushed back to the room, and I limped after him.

What happened? The competition was over, but he went to the judges to plead my case. While he was pleading, I was praying, and I know my mom was somewhere praying also. After ten long minutes, he came back and said the judges agreed to hear my speech. I gave it all I had. I showed passion, quoted statistics. I used hand gestures all while limping up and down the stage. By the time my mom caught up with me, I had completed my speech. She asked how things went, and I told her I did the best I could.

After a few weeks, I went to see my guidance counselor for the results. He sat me down in his office and explained that the judges had already chosen a winner before I came. I hung my head in disappointment. He went on to say because they thought my speech was so much better, the fair thing to do was to award each of us a scholarship. I couldn't believe my ears! Who would believe that I won a competition after it was declared to be over? When I ran home to tell my family the good news, my mom nearly shed tears. She knew, and I knew, that God had come through again.

It is difficult for the pastor in me to resist the biblical analogy from this incident. By that I mean, when Jesus was crucified on the cross, He was pinned there by nails. These nails were much larger than the one I stepped on that held my foot in place. Many thought His mission had come to a disappointing end. Jesus raised His head and cried, "Tetelestai" which means, "It is finished." He died without establishing the earthly empire

His disciples wanted. His followers' hopes were shattered. On the other hand, we who know the rest of the story would have loved to remind them of the promise. If we were there on Friday afternoon, we would pull them aside and whisper in their ears, "It may be finished, but it ain't over!" Three days later, He rose again. The nails couldn't keep Him down.

What nails are holding you back? For many, it's the fear of failure. One survey found that one in three Americans are scared of failure.[2] A singular failure can injure your sense of identity, shaking your confidence and faith in yourself. What's more, repeated failures can cause one to become indifferent and unmotivated, starting projects and not finishing them, knowing about a problem but lacking the energy to tackle it. This notorious phobia can also lead to underperforming because you are content to simply coast, which carries little risk and can be accomplished with minimal effort.

If you have been wounded by failure, here are some recommendations to assist you:

Lesson #1: Try Again

> *Don't be afraid to start over. This time, you're not starting from scratch. You're starting from experience.*
>
> -Unknown

One of the secrets to success is failure. That may sound strange, nonetheless it is true. Rarely do people get things done perfectly the first time around due to the learning curve inherent in executing most tasks and activities. To be sure, performance and skills improve with repetition, resulting in better efficiency, reducing hesitation, and minimizing mistakes. A point of fact, research by psychologist K. Anders Ericsson suggests it takes ten thousand hours of practice to become an elite performer. It appears then, that failure is a prerequisite for excellence. I like NBA Coach Rick Patino's appellation for failure, he calls it fertilizer! What you learn by examining mistakes helps you maximize your fruitfulness. Therefore, try again.

Lesson #2: Take Risks

A fear of failure can make you risk-adverse. You are tempted to always play it safe. But the biggest risk is not taking one. Executives of Fortune 500 companies have applied this principle often. Amazon CEO, Jeff Bezos, is an avid proponent of taking calculated risks. "I've made billions of dollars of failures at Amazon.com. Literally...None of those things are fun, but also, they don't matter. What matters is companies that don't continue to experiment or embrace failure eventually get in the position where the only thing they can do is make a Hail Mary bet at the end of their corporate existence.[3]

Steve Jobs talked about a call he made when he was only 12 years old. He found the phone number of Bill Hewlett in the phonebook. Bill was the co-founder of the Hewlett-Packard Company. Steve dialed the number and Bill actually picked up. Young Jobs requested any available parts for a frequency counter he was building. Impressed with young Steve, Bill gave him the parts and offered him a summer job assembling frequency counters. After becoming his own electronics and computer giant, Steve said, "Most people never pick up the phone and call. Most people never ask. That's what separates, sometimes, the people who do things and the people that just dream about them. You gotta act. You gotta be willing to fail. You've gotta be willing to crash and burn. If you're afraid of failing, you won't get very far."[4]

See failure for what it is—a part of life. Smith College issues a Certificate of Failure to those who graduate from its Fail Well program. It reads, the recipient is "hereby authorized to screw up, bomb, or otherwise fail at one or more relationships, hook-ups, friendships, emails or text, papers, exams, classes, extracurricular activities or any other choices or decisions associated with college herein wherefore and forevermore... and still be a totally worthy, utterly excellent human being."

Lesson #3: Avoid Binary Thinking

If your thinking is limited, your life will be limited.

-Joel Osteen

Many approach life with the binary mindset of one problem, one solution. In actuality, there can be a hundred ways to deal with one problem. I thought that if I didn't make it to the competition in time, I would lose. I came after the competition was over and won. I thought there could only be one winner. To show fairness, the judges awarded two scholarships. What if I had given up because it seemed like my situation was hopeless—hobbling in the eleventh hour through an unfamiliar campus? Failure is not a reason to give up. It's an opportunity to become creative and develop innovative solutions to problems that defeated binary thinkers.

Application Exercises

1. Write out the words on the Certificate of Failure issued by Smith College.

   _____

   _____

   _____

   _____

   _____

   _____

2. Have you ever had to come out of your comfort zone? What were the results?

   _____

   _____

   _____

   _____

   _____

3. Describe a time in your life when the options seemed few and someone came up with a creative solution.

   _____

   _____

   _____

   _____

   _____

The people who influence you
are the people who believe in you.

-Henry Drummond

Battle Lessons from the Fire

When you react, you are giving away your power.
When you respond, you are staying in control of yourself.

-Bob Proctor

CHAPTER 3

had never seen flames that high and that close. We had a drop ceiling, and I didn't know drop ceilings could melt. It did that day. It seemed like the burning flames reached up and grabbed fistfuls at a time. Chunks of plastic were falling from above, all around the stove. If that wasn't bad enough, I looked to my left and saw that I had bigger problems.

It was one of those days. I was determined to create my own girl- cave, she-shed, retreat in our kitchen. I was about 16 years old. Most 16-year-old girls spend their days talking about boys, fashion, and movies. However, my grandmother suffered a stroke in Haiti. My mother immediately flew down and brought her back to our home in Miami. My mother hired aides, but most of them only spoke English making it impossible for them to understand my grandmother's now slurred French and Creole. Who had the most flexible schedule at the time? You guessed it, me.

Every day, I would come home to sit in my grandmother's room, translate what she needed to her aide, then relieve the aide at the end of her shift. I cooked for her, fed her, and bathed her. I even helped her practice walking again. Every afternoon, we would hit the sidewalk. She would take her cane to help drag her paralyzed right leg along. I walked with her at a reduced pace of course, and along the way I would tell her jokes and make her laugh. She was an active and successful businesswoman back home, and I'd like to think those moments of levity helped her to cope with her new way of life.

Well, it was the end of the day. I had put my grandmother to bed and decided it was time to relax. I was going to make one of my favorite dishes and eat it while watching one of my favorite shows. Then I got the brilliant idea to combine the two intentions. Why go into the living room when I can carry a TV into the kitchen? Mind you, it wouldn't be a flat-screen TV, but a large, clunky, heavy CRT television—with nobs and all. I lifted it out of one of the bedrooms and placed it on the kitchen counter.

I pulled out some plantains, green and yellow. I was going to make a dish called banan peze! I would peel the plantains and chop them into four pieces. I would press those pieces between the plantain skin, then soak the pressed pieces in salt-water. I poured an inch of oil in the pan and fried the pieces a few at a time. When I was done, I reached over to turn off the fire. I pulled up a chair, turned my back to the stove, faced the television, placed the plate of banan peze on my lap, and began to eat and watch TV.

Moments later, I heard a sudden WOOSH. I turned around to see flames coming from the pan and hitting the ceiling. When I looked at the stove knob, I realized I hadn't turned it all the way. Instead of turning the stove off, I turned it to high! The bigger problem was, the TV was now on the kitchen counter close to the flames. I knew if the flames met the TV, a mini explosion would follow. I took the TV from the counter and placed it away on the floor. I then ran outside where my older sister was hanging out with her boyfriend. I shattered their tranquil moment by bursting through the door yelling, "The kitchen's on fire, the kitchen's on fire!" They ran in and were stunned to see the great flames. Her boyfriend hurried to smother the flames. They took wet towels and threw them over the pan. Eventually, they managed to put out the fire. But now the kitchen walls were black from the smoke. The flames left gaping holes in the drop ceiling. At least, we had stopped the fire from taking over the entire kitchen.

My mother pulled into the driveway a few hours later. I ran to meet her outside. I jumped into the car, and her first words were, "What happened?" I stuttered and stammered, then finally pushed out the entire story at record speed. I remember her listening in silence. The entire time, she had a look of disbelief on her face. I began crying and apologizing over and over again for almost burning down the kitchen. I knew she would never trust me again to take care of my grandmother. In between sobs, I heard my mother calmly say her first words: "Well, you're going back in tomorrow." I thought I would certainly be banned from the kitchen for at least a week. But she repeated, "You're going back in tomorrow to keep cooking for your grandmother."

The next day, she went to work. I came home from school and stood in the middle of the kitchen surrounded by smoke-tainted walls. The ceiling above me was a ceiling made of jagged holes. I pulled out a pot and began cooking my grandmother's next dish. I was scared. I was afraid I would forget to turn off the stove again. Still, I had to feed grandma, so I pushed through it. My mother knew the only way to drive out the fear of messing up again was to get back in the saddle.

Best-selling author Robert Glazer wrote, "The reality is that what we often need the most is to face that exact thing that just caused the pain – and we need to do it quickly. This way we can move past and through it and make a new memory, overriding the bad experience with a new one before it has the opportunity to set in too deep."

Slowly but surely, I got over my fear. My grandmother and I were back to laughing on the sidewalk. I bathed her. I put her in bed. And, yes, I made her dinner.

How do you manage your home? Do you supervise employees? Are you responsible for a team? For some of you reading this book, the answer is yes. For others, the answer is no. Although that may not be the case now, you may be responsible for a team in the future. How will you respond when, for some reason, a destabilizing difficulty arrives on your doorstep?

As a pastor, I sometimes must deal with errant members. When we meet, I first try to do for them what my mother did for me. Mom showed me, despite the mishap, my behavior did not change who she knew me to be. If the nature of the offense is so severe it requires some form of disciplinary action, I still communicate to them love and concern for their well-being by checking on them through follow-up calls, texts, and visits.

How you respond as a leader to difficulties can make all the difference, because it can make or break your team. Ideally, spend less time considering the cause of the event and more time in your response to it. Although there is plenty of merit in considering whether the problem was inevitable, determining if someone was distracted, ascertaining if procedures were properly followed, none of it changes the situation at hand. Therefore, spend exponentially more time on how to improve the current situation. What steps can you take now? Collaborate with your team and figure out ways to minimize the damage and maximize the potential opportunities for growth and understanding.

As a leader who must pilot your team through turbulence, learn how to put people at ease. Be approachable, which is unlike the ruthless and demanding CEOs popular on the big screen. Think of Margaret Tate from The Proposal. She's an impossible-to-please editor-in-chief of a major New York publishing company who blackmails her assistant to get what she wants. J Jonah Jameson is Peter Parker's micromanaging boss at the Daily Bugle. He vilifies Spider-Man and takes Peter Parker's pay without remorse. The worse of them all, and most hilarious, in my opinion, is Miranda Priestly from The Devil Wears Prada. She's cold, heartless, and a master of psychological games that keep everyone around her unsettled. She can ruin an entire fashion showcase simply by pursing her lips. Despite these images, the most successful CEOs in today's workplace are well-adjusted leaders.

Research confirms extraordinary leaders have a combination of gravitas and emotional intelligence. What exactly is gravitas? You may think gravitas describes a person who is physically imposing. That is not how it's depicted by the senior executives surveyed in a study conducted by the Center for Talent Innovation. Gravitas means that one possesses a combination of knowledge, confidence, and knowing how to get buy-in under difficult circumstances. Notice how the first two qualities complement one another. You can be confident because you know your stuff cold and can go six questions deep in your domains of knowledge.[5]

As for the second attribute, nearly 90 percent of what sets high performers apart from peers with similar technical skills and knowledge is Emotional Intelligence.[6] Emotionally Intelligent leaders demonstrate grace under pressure. They accomplish this in part through self-awareness. They've made the effort to know themselves, their strengths and flaws. They're cognizant of their tendencies, what makes them upset, and what motivates them. Regulating their emotions and knowing how to manage and influence the emotions of others around them is their hallmark. These leaders know how to deliver feedback. When people speak to them, they listen well by paying attention to how things are being said and not just what is being said.

A popular story is told about a group of frogs traveling through the woods. Two of them fell into a deep pit. When the other frogs saw how deep the pit was, they told the two frogs that they were as good as dead. The two frogs ignored the comments and tried to jump up out of the pit with all their might. The other frogs at the mouth of the pit kept hollering at them to stop, that they were as good as dead. Finally, one of the frogs took heed to what the other frogs were saying and gave up. He fell down and died.

The other frog continued to jump as hard as he could. Once again, the crowd of frogs yelled at him to stop the pain and just die. He jumped even harder and finally, with one valiant jump, he made it out of the pit. You see this frog was deaf and unable to hear what the others were saying. He thought they were encouraging him the entire time and that made all the difference. How you communicate is often as important as what you are communicating. Furthermore, while negative words can kill the spirit and the will to fight, encouraging words can help the down and out become the up and out.

When you have to maneuver through an unexpected problem, focus on solutions, draw from your expertise while encouraging collaboration. Regulate your emotions and that of those around you. Finally, remember to season your speech with wisdom and encouragement.

I still think about my mother's response that day and how it affected me. It's a marvelous feeling to be restored and not replaced. Generally speaking, most situations and people are redeemable. If you address issues with healthy, balanced, and effective practices, people usually respond with loyalty and dedication.

Application Exercises

1. Have you ever been given a second chance? What did it feel like?

_____

_____

_____

_____

_____

2. Think of a problem you are facing now. Summarize what caused it in one sentence. Write a paragraph about possible solutions.

_____

_____

_____

_____

_____

3. Visualization exercise: What does your workplace or situation look like when the problem is resolved?

_____

_____

_____

_____

_____

*There will come a time when you believe
everything is finished. That will be the beginning.*

-Louis L'Amour

Battle Lessons from the Call Part 1

CHAPTER 4

"You're never going to make it." "You'll never get hired."
"You'll never get married."

These were the most popular comments I heard when I announced my big decision that I was going to enter the ministry. For a while, it looked like their predictions would come true. After all, the Seventh-day Adventist Church has only a handful of female pastors in North America today. They had even less in the 90s. The odds of me getting hired were slim to none.

I did not begin ministerial training out of a casual curiosity. As a matter of fact, I had the early impression the journey would be quite difficult. Accordingly, when I sensed God's call, I spent weeks praying and fasting about it. "God, is this really what You want me to do? Show me a sign. I will keep this conviction to myself. Make someone come to me unexpectedly and tell me I should be a pastor."

It was 1996 and my two-year scholarship to MDCC was just about finished. I had a choice. I could move to Huntsville, AL and enroll in the Theology program at Oakwood College (now University), or remain in Miami. If I chose the latter, I could transfer my credits to Florida International University (FIU) and major in Biology. Attending FIU was the most convenient option because I wouldn't have to move out of state. In addition, I applied for a new higher-paying job only five minutes from my house. If I passed their pre-employment tests, I was hired.

I took the tests and I passed with flying colors! Now, it

seemed like a no-brainer. Living at home was rent-free, my new job would easily pay for tuition and the combination of these two factors would afford me quite a bit of discretionary income. I worked out an understanding with my parents that I would go to work full-time and attend school part-time. My plans were set.

The new company notified me by phone that I was hired, and I could barely contain my enthusiasm! They then instructed me to look out for another call regarding the start date of training for the position. As a matter of course, I handed in my letter of resignation at my current job and waited with great anticipation for the second call.

A week went by, and no one called. I figured it wouldn't do any harm if I picked up the phone and gave them a call. When the receptionist answered, I was asked for my name and put on hold. When she returned to the line, I was told they would get back with me soon with the start date. A couple more weeks went by and still no one called. I called them again and was given the same message.

In the meanwhile, summer was about to end, and Fall Semester was about to begin. It so happened, one weekday I was hanging out with a friend at her office. Starting to get concerned about the delay, I decided to call the company one more time. The receptionist answered the phone, and we went through the usual routine. I was asked for my name and put on hold. This time, however, the person came back and said, "We do not have any record of you."

"Excuse me," I protested, "Please check again."

She did and then returned saying, "We don't even have a file for you. Perhaps you failed our pre-employment tests."

"Oh no! I did very well on the tests," I said, baffled. "The examiner complimented me on my scores."

"Well, I'm sorry. But we don't know who you are. We did not hire you," she said, agitated, then hung up the phone.

My heart sank. The phone was still in my hand when I thought, "This can't be happening." I could not go back to my old job. The job that would help pay for classes at FIU was no longer available. How could this happen? I felt like my life came to a standstill.

I can't say I'm proud of what happened next. Would you believe I began to crank-call the company. Whenever someone picked up the phone, I'd make the weirdest, spontaneous, high-pitched, animated sounds then quickly hang up.

Round One

Me: (dialing)

Them: Hello

Me: Wee wee wee keee keee wayaya blah blah blee (hang up)

Round Two (10 seconds later)

Me: (dialing)

Them: Hello

Me: Wusha wusha wusha, pizita patootoo, zibiday (hang up)

Round Three (10 seconds later)

You get the picture. I did this several times and as my friend watched me make each call, all she could do was shake her head in disbelief. I got the frustration out of my system after about the fifth go-around. I sat there wearing a smirk on my face, with crossed arms, feeling smug.

Evidently, I had underestimated the power of caller ID.

Suddenly, the phone rang. We stared at each other with widened eyes and mouths open. Then my friend picked up the phone and answered in her best professional voice... "XXXX Psychiatry, how may I help you?" It was the company calling back asking for the culprit. My friend denied knowing anything about crank calls coming from this number. It happened that she worked at a psych office, so that worked in my favor. As far as the company was concerned, it could have been a patient who had managed to break away from supervision. After my friend hung up, I flopped back in my chair, breathed a sigh of relief and thought to myself "Bullet dodged!"

I went home and had a lot to think about that day. God was making Himself clear that I was going to Oakwood.

Stop waiting for someone else
to give you permission to prosper.

-Unknown

After I decided to go to Oakwood, what I had prayed for happened. I finished a routine presentation during the morning service at church. As usual, I returned in the afternoon for the youth program. I was walking through the sanctuary doors when one of the members came charging in my direction. He grabbed me by both arms and, with excitement, said, "You should be a pastor!" Wait a minute. Time out. I prayed for this very moment. Though it was finally happening, it felt hollow because God had already spoken.

I've discovered too many people are waiting for permission from others to follow their dreams. If you are waiting for people to validate your dreams, to tell you you're good enough or smart enough, you won't get very far. What you are doing is a subtle form of procrastination that continually pushes your start date to somewhere in the future that never comes. Making big changes and pursuing your passion is not for the faint of heart. It's much easier just to drift through life doing the bare minimum. The problem with that is, you may end up living a life full of regrets.

Research shows people regret things they didn't do more than the things they did, even if things they did turn out poorly. It turns out actions cause more pain in the short-term, but inactions are regretted more in the long run.[7] Some people are waiting to be discovered by the right person who will feel compelled to invest in them. However, people who get what they want out of life invest in themselves. They don't wait to be discovered. They seize the day and get to work.

Application Exercises

1. What are you passionate about? Do you prefer working with people, things, or information? Rank them in order.

   People

   Information

   things

   _____

   _____

   _____

2. What skills do you need to develop to be successful in your chosen field?

   Technology teaching

   Strategies

   _____

   _____

   _____

3. What resources will you need to pursue your passion?

   Coaching/training

   _____

   _____

   _____

*It does not matter how slowly you go
as long as you do not stop.*

-Confucius

Battle Lessons
from the Call
Part II

CHAPTER 5

I loved my time at Oakwood College. From 1996 to 2000, I met people from all over the world and made friends for life, including my best friend. My professors set high expectations. I took courses, including Greek, Hebrew, Ancient Near Eastern Literature, Church History, Systematic Theology, Old and New Testament, preaching and pastoral counseling. Not to mention the worship was amazing!!! I did especially well with languages and was a Greek tutor. I relished coming up with original mnemonics to help the students recall and retain Greek vocabulary and grammar. After a four- year matriculation, my experience at Oakwood stirred up an insatiable thirst for knowledge and did wonders for my spiritual growth. But now, it was graduation time.

This is how the system typically worked. Seventh-day Adventist churches are organized into Conferences. Conference officials would visit campus to interview graduating seniors for potential employment. If you were hired, we called it getting "picked up." If you were picked up, one of two things would happen: The Conference assigned you to pastor a church. The other option was to send you to seminary and pay for your Master of Divinity degree. Sometimes you would be sent to a church for a few years and then sent to seminary.

I went to every interview. I was often told they are not hiring at the moment. However, my male classmates would walk out of their interviews with the same conference official with job offers or seminary sponsorships. Those were disheartening moments. I paid out of pocket for my undergraduate degree. Without a job offer or sponsorship, I would have to take out more loans to pay for my seminary education as well.

Courage doesn't always roar. Sometimes courage is the little voice at the end of the day that says I'll try again tomorrow.

Mary Anne Radmacher

I moved to Berrien Springs, MI and spent three years at Andrews University Theological Seminary. I met my husband, a sponsored student from New Jersey, in my final year. We got engaged and planned to get married after graduation. During my final semester at Andrews, Allegheny East Conference sent a representative to the campus named Freddie Russell. He is a top leadership guru and was pastoring one of the most dynamic Adventist Churches in Maryland. I received calls from several classmates throughout the day telling me a recruiter was on campus that I should meet. Even so, I had gone down this road before, and I did not want to go through another rejection. I wasn't making any special preparations to meet him. I had resigned myself to the fact that I would get married and move to New Jersey with my husband. There, I would get a job, any job, to pay off my mounting student loans. Later in the day, I received a call saying Pastor Russell had requested to meet with me, specifically. I was skeptical, but I went to the interview.

What an interview it was! We felt God's presence in the meeting. He was looking for fresh ideas. I shared with him fresh ideas I implemented while ministering on campus. We were practically finishing each other's sentences. Then it happened. He did not wait until after the meeting. He didn't promise he would give me a call later. Right there and then he said, "Paula, I want you to come work with me." Wow! After all this time...after how the previous interviews had gone, I had no intention of even being in this room at this time.

I remembered the speech I gave graduation weekend at Oakwood just a few years prior. It was the Friday night consecration service. Normally, it's the student body chaplain who gives the response to the guest speaker's charge. However, earlier in the week, the student body president called my dorm room and said he felt impressed to ask me to give the response instead. I was surprised. He insisted, and I consented. The day came, and I stood before the student body dressed in my regalia. In front of a sea of fellow graduates, parents, administrators, and faculty, I talked about our tumultuous journey through exams and financial clearance the past four years. Then I concluded my speech by reciting these words that seemed to have been our unofficial motto:

> *When things go wrong as they sometimes will,*
> *When the road you're trudging seems all up hill,*
> *When the funds are low and the debts are high*
> *And you want to smile, but you have to sigh,*
> *When care is pressing you down a bit,*
>
> *Rest if you must, but don't you quit.*
> *Life is strange with its twists and turns*
> *As every one of us sometimes learns*
>
> *And many a failure comes about*
> *When he might have won had he stuck it out.*
> *Don't give up though the pace seems slow—*
>
> *You may succeed with another blow.*
> *Success is failure turned inside out—*
> *The silver tint of the clouds of doubt,*
>
> *And you never can tell just how close you are,*
> *It may be near when it seems so far*
>
> *So stick to the fight when you're hardest hit—*
> *It's when things seem worst that you must not quit!*

The speech was met with a standing ovation. At the time, I thought I was reflecting on the past. In retrospect, I believe God was giving me marching orders for the future. Had I not stuck it out and given it one more blow, this moment with Freddie never would have happened.

He told me he was looking to add a female pastor on his staff at Miracle Temple in Baltimore. There was only one caveat. He could promise me work, but he could not guarantee me pay. Essentially, he wanted to put my skills on display. If I did well, then it's possible AEC would offer me a full-time position.

I didn't know what this meant for my engagement. I would have to move to Maryland, stay with a friend, and hope to get hired full-time. My fiancé was extremely supportive. He said to me, if that is what God is calling me to do at this time, then I should do it.

It was 2004. I left my fiancé at Andrews University and moved to Maryland. My friend, Pastor Darriel Hoy, with a heart of generosity and grace offered me a place to stay.

Pastor Russell had secured funding and given me a sizeable monthly stipend. I went to Miracle Temple Church and received a royal welcome. My parents flew in from Miami for my installation. I was the first female pastor in the church's history.

I had the pleasure of working alongside Pastor Russell and Pastor Alex Royes. Our pastoral team formed a perfect trifecta. We complemented each other well. I loved the church and my ministry there flourished quickly. Four months later, just as Pastor Russell's funding for me ran out, AEC offered me a full-time job in New Jersey!

Subsequently, I left Miracle Temple, got married, and moved to New Jersey. I was installed as Assistant Pastor of The SDA

Church of the Oranges to work with senior pastor Samuel G. Campbell. I was their first female pastor. Later, I was assigned my own church. I pastored the First SDA Church of Montclair in Montclair, NJ. Now, I am the Pastor of Ebenezer SDA Church—a 550-member congregation in Long Island, NY. This is my fourth congregation. Everywhere I have been assigned, I have been the church's first female pastor.

In Long Island, I pastor the church the Conference President's family attends. He enjoys telling people, "That's my pastor." In 2016, I received job offers from three separate Conferences. I am humbled by the fact I went from being warned by well-intentioned people not to enter Pastoral Ministry, "You won't get a job...You'll never get married," to choosing which job offer I wanted to accept and married my seminary sweetheart, the brilliant and handsome Dr. Smith Olivier.

A man's gift makes room for him
and brings him before great men.

-Proverbs 18:16 NASB

Right after my first installation weekend, I went to the office to meet with Pastor Russell for orientation and to receive my assignments. It was there he shared with me how he sought me out. He spoke with my professors who told him I was an excellent student. He spoke with my campus mentor, Pastor Clifford Jones. He was told I was one of the top preachers on campus. I guess something about my preaching appealed to people. I didn't know I was being noticed. I simply took counsel from my professors. They encouraged us to take every speaking engagement when possible and within reason, so we can sharpen our skills. I preached somewhere in the country practically every other weekend. The exposure helped me to hone my preaching skills. What valuable counsel! The reviews he received led Pastor Russell to want to meet with me in person.

When Pastor Russell told me about the role his "background check" played in offering me a job, I realized you must bloom where you are planted. Don't wait until you get offered your first job, large church, major assignment, or a prestigious platform. Hone your craft now, and practice excellence every day.

Appreciate where you are, what you have, and improve upon it. Otherwise, it's easy to fall into the "if only" mode. If only I had a nicer car, I'd give people a ride. If only I had a bigger house, I would invite someone over for lunch. If only I had a bigger paycheck, I would give to charity. You don't have to be rich and affluent to be hospitable or generous. That is the inverse of what the Bible teaches. "Well done, you good and faithful servant!" said his master. "You have been faithful in managing small amounts, so I will put you in charge of large amounts. Come on in and share my happiness!" Matthew 25:23 GNT. Those who are faithful with few, get rewarded with many.

If you don't appreciate what you have, you'll start comparing it with what someone else has. Be careful. Comparing leads to complaining. Instead of working on the one talent you know you possess, you'll be busy complaining about someone who appears to have several talents. Improve what you have instead of wasting time and energy desiring someone else's possessions.

Comparing also has the unintended consequence of creating competitors out of the people you envy, a fact to which they may be completely oblivious. More than that, competing with those around you is antithetical to your goals. When you compete with others, they become the standard and the measure of success. As you beat them, the satisfaction may tempt you to rest on your laurels. A better proposition than competing with others is to compete with yourself and nobody else. Strive to be better today than you were yesterday. Beat your best time, your best score, your best performance, because chasing your unrealized potential is a surer path to greatness.

Application Exercises

1. How much time are you prepared to spend on your goal? Schedule time(s) in your day to work on your career goal.

_____

_____

_____

_____

_____

2. Do an internet search. List the associations, journals, magazines, blogs, and podcasts relative to your field of interest.

_____

_____

_____

3. When is the next opportunity you'll have to exercise your talent? Do it even if you're nervous. No matter how things go, return to this exercise and right about it below.

_____

_____

_____

_____

_____

*The great use of life is to spend it
for something that will outlast it.*

-William James

Battle Lessons
from Legacy

CHAPTER 6

When I was in high school, I volunteered to tutor elementary school students in an underserved community.

It was an opportunity to give them one-on-one attention to help them improve their grades. During a specific lesson, I needed to ask the student, "What do you want to be when you grow up?" Most of them gave the typical answers—Doctor, Lawyer, Engineer. At any rate, on more than one occasion, I heard an answer that caught me off guard. A child would say, "I want to be a manager at McDonald's!" They said it with such pride. I thought to myself, "That is your dream? What happened to aiming high?"

Each time, I gently probed to see why their aspiration was so pedestrian. The story was the same. The child had an older sibling who was a manager at McDonald's. It seemed to them that their brother or sister had the most money in their home. As a result, becoming a fast food employee was not a starter job or summer job. It was their goal. There are plenty of good people who work entry-level jobs and make an honest living. Be that as it may, it's a problem when you're asked to shoot for the stars, and you aim for the ballpark of minimum wage. Their answers were telling. They aspired to be fast food workers because that is what they were exposed to.

Steven Covey teaches everything is created twice, first in the mind and then in reality. "There's a mental or first creation, and a physical or second creation, to all things." I believe if our children are not exposed to greatness, their dreams may be diluted. They may never see themselves as who they can truly become. On the other hand, exposing children to legacy can broaden their horizons.

A hero is someone who has given his or her life
to something bigger than oneself.

-Joseph Campbell

Monuments serve multiple purposes and one of them is to honor great achievements. The school system often takes kids on tours because of its positive impact on spectators. How many field trips did you take as a kid? Chances are, something you were exposed to changed or inspired you. Perhaps something you saw, the memorial of a heroic event or an astonishing achievement, infused you with hope and enthusiasm. Legacy can do that.

There is a statue of my father in Savanah, GA. It's in Jefferson Square. Whenever I see it, I am infused with enthusiasm.Both of my parents were born in Haiti. My dad was a proud Haitian businessman and an American Citizen. My siblings and I were born in Brooklyn, NY. Growing up as a Haitian American is a unique experience because you straddle two powerful worlds, trying to live Haitian values in an American context. Haitians are generally more conservative and traditional. Respect, hospitality, and education are highly esteemed. As a young person, your number one job is your education. We have the type of parents who when we receive 99% on a paper will ask us, "What happened to the 1%?" You know the type. When it comes to education, there are no excuses. In school and in life, you are always expected to give it your best.

My father, Daniel Fils-Aimé Sr., seemed to take those

expectations to another level. He was full of enterprise, ingenuity, and boldness. He started a successful business in Miami, FL. In addition to heading his own transportation company, he became a community leader and activist. He dreamed big and expected others around him to do the same.

Daniel believed in civic engagement and knew that being part of an organization multiplies your influence. He was co-founder of the Haitian American Chamber of Commerce of Florida (HACCOF), served on the Miami-Dade International Trade Consortium Advisory Board, a board member of the Center for Haitian Studies (CHS), and founder and Chairman of the Haitian American Historical Society (HAHS). As a successful entrepreneur, he traveled the world. The Savannah Herald stated it most eloquently in their August 8, 2018 issue: "Today, many in the top echelons of power in the United States, and some other countries regard Daniel as a friend. Over the years, these included being at meetings with President Barak Obama, President Bill Clinton, First Lady Hillary Clinton, former Governor Jeb Bush, Mother Theresa, Billy Graham, Yasser Arafat and many more." I still remember him telling me about his meeting with President Nelson Mandela.

For my father, his achievements were part and parcel of his Haitian identity. He stood on the shoulders of the great men and women of Haitian History. Through HAHS, he realized one of his cherished goals—the building of the Chasseur Volunteers monument in Savannah, GA. It was there over 500 free Haitian men fought for the United States to gain their independence during the American Revolution. This project was my dad's brainchild, so the sculptor used my father's image to make one of the soldiers. He's the kneeling soldier (see appendix).

I had never heard of this battle. It was not mentioned in my

American History textbooks. The only connection between Haiti and the United States I ever saw publicized were images of Haitian refugees desperately trying to get to America. But how many people know we had already been here—not as paupers, but as protectors of liberty? My dad knew. Plenty of native Haitians know this because it was in their textbooks.

I remember sitting for a standardized test in elementary school. It had one question pertaining to Haiti, and the correct answer was listed as "the poorest country in the Western Hemisphere." We act according to our self-image, and the one presented to Haitian Americans while growing up in America is often difficult to tolerate. We don't see ourselves as beleaguered and destitute. We are confident and proud of who we are.

Unfortunately, I lost my father on July 31, 2018. The City of North Miami, FL passed a resolution making the day of his funeral, August 12th, Daniel Fils-Aimé Sr. Day. A framed copy of that resolution hangs in my office. Dealing with his death has been difficult, but his legacy persuaded me to search for more gems in Haitian history omitted in my Eurocentric education. What I discovered was a treasure-trove of inspiration.

I began with analyzing the Haitian Revolution (1791–1804). Mention Toussaint Louverture and many will say under his leadership Haiti defeated Napoleon Bonaparte. However, Louveture and the Haitian people defeated three world empires to achieve liberty—the French, the Spanish, and the British. The Haitian Revolution was not a spontaneous revolt that got lucky. Its success required strategy as well as bravery. The Haitian rebels Toussaint, Biassou, and Jean-Francois evaluated the political climate brought about by the French Revolution and used it to their advantage. Our war with Napoleon forced the Louisiana Purchase practically doubling the size of the United States.[8]

After gaining its independence, Haiti supported emancipation across the globe. President Alexandre Pétion actively supported Simon Bolivar, the hero of South America's independence. He provided Bolivar with men, money, and ammunition in return for a promise to abolish slavery in South America.[9] Haitian state vessels captured several slave-trading vessels bound for neighboring colonies with captives taken from Africa. In these cases, the captives were liberated and allowed to remain in Haiti, and the ships were sent on to their destinations, usually with their crews but without their human cargoes.[10]

If my father were alive today, I would sit with him and ask him to tell me more about our great nation. I can imagine the excitement in his eyes. I can see the joy on his face as we explore our shared knowledge about Haiti together. I probably still don't know as much as he knew. Nevertheless, I am grateful that the passion he displayed for his people led me to know more. I cherish this new knowledge and love sharing it.

Legacy is not leaving something for people.
It's leaving something in people.

-Peter Strople

After winning several archery contests, the young and rather boastful champion challenged a Zen master who was renowned for his skill as an archer. The young man demonstrated remarkable technical proficiency when he hit a distant bull's eye on his first try, and then split that arrow with his second shot. "There," he said to the old man, "see if you can match that!" Undisturbed, the master did not draw his bow, but rather motioned for the young archer to follow him up the mountain.

Curious about the old fellow's intentions, the champion followed him high into the mountain until they reached a deep chasm spanned by a rather flimsy and shaky log. Calmly stepping out onto the middle of the unsteady and certainly perilous bridge, the old master picked a faraway tree as a target, drew his bow, and fired a clean, direct hit. "Now it is your turn," he said as he gracefully stepped back onto the safe ground. Staring with terror into the seemingly bottomless and beckoning abyss, the young man could not force himself to step out onto the log, no less shoot at a target. "You have much skill with your bow," the master said, sensing his challenger's predicament, "but you have little skill with the mind that lets loose the shot." When the conditions changed, he became unnerved, lost confidence, and retreated.

To accomplish a goal of this magnitude, Daniel had to persist under constantly shifting conditions. He was able to succeed anyway because of passion for his people and perseverance. My father built his business from the ground up. He had to make tough calls and overcome resistance. He used the same skills to get the monument built. Monuments help shape public memory. Daniel knew the Savannah Project would challenge the predominate understanding of many about Haiti and its people. The way forward was not always easy. But sometimes opposition is validation you are doing something significant.

If you want to build a legacy that lasts, you need more than talent and business acumen. You need stamina. Don't let disappointments distract you. Dust yourself off and press on.

I think about the Nobel Laureates my father had the pleasure of meeting. Mother Teresa was a Roman Catholic nun and founder of the Missionaries of Charity. She spent most of her life in India where she became famous for dedicating her life to care for the lepers, the homeless, and the dying in the slums of

Kolkata. Through the Missionaries of Charity, she established homes all over the world for the sick, orphaned children, lepers, and the disabled. Although at the outset, she wanted to help the sick, she didn't know how to treat diseases. To improve her skills, she enrolled in an intensive medical training with the American Medical Missionary Sisters in Patna, India. If she ran out of money, that didn't stop her. She begged until she collected enough to continue her work. When she couldn't afford a building, she taught children how to write by drawing in the dirt. She had little help when she began. But after she passed away, over 4,000 sisters, an associated brotherhood of 300 members, and over 100,000 volunteers were operating 610 missions in 123 countries trying to continue her legacy. Her passion helped her persevere through precarious and unexpected situations.

Nelson Rolihlahla Mandel was South Africa's first Black president. He spent thirty years in prison for fighting against Apartheid. He wrote in his autobiography,

To be an African in South Africa means that one is politicized from the moment of one's birth, whether one acknowledges it or not. An African child is born in an Africans Only hospital, taken home in an Africans Only bus, lives in an Africans Only area, and attends Africans Only schools, if he attends school at all. When he grows up, he can hold Africans Only jobs, rent a house in Africans Only townships, ride Africans Only trains, and be stopped at any time of the day or night and be ordered to produce a pass, failing which he will be arrested and thrown in jail.[11]

He helped organize protests, marches, and boycotts. When Mandela heard the government was planning to ban his political party (the African National Congress), he developed ways for them to operate underground. He was arrested. On at least six separate occasions, he received conditional offers in exchange for his freedom. None of those offers would end apartheid. He refused them all. After denying another offer, he wrote a letter. His daughter Zindzi read it to a crowd of supporters at Jabulani Stadium. Mandela stated that although he cherished his own freedom, he cared even more about theirs. He went on to state, "Your freedom and mine cannot be separated." While in prison, he persisted in negotiating peace with the government. As a result, he won the Nobel Peace Prize while still incarcerated. After twenty-seven years behind bars, he was released. Apartheid was dismantled, and Nelson Mandela became South Africa's first democratically elected president.

How did he survive those years in incarceration? His letters from prison give us some insight. He wrote to his family "perseverance is the key to success...Remember that hope is a powerful weapon even when all else is lost."[12] Our lessons on legacy underscore the following: the necessity of passion and perseverance. Passion and perseverance are indispensable for those who want to leave a positive impact on the world. Passion and perseverance help you absorb the hits to your dreams and encourage you to press on.

Secondly, think long term. Monuments keep these inspiring narratives from fading into obscurity. Seeing them prompts us to rehearse the story. When these accounts are shared, they leave deposits in the imagination that can bear fruit. How is your legacy coming along? If you can't leave behind a statue, you can leave behind a story. What will others say of you when you are no longer around? Did you leave this world better than how you found it? Think long-term. Remember these words:

"Someone is sitting in the shade today because someone planted a tree a long time ago."

-Warren Buffet

Application Exercises

1. Describe what your ideal life looks like.

Married with kids and grandkids
a career in university getting
ready to retire and then be
a mentor and or coach to other
teachers or people in general

2. Have you ever been inspired by a trip or a tour? What
about it impacted you?

3. What is the legacy you want to leave behind? What do
you want to be said about you?

I want my life to impact the
people around me and be remem
bered as resilient and inspiring.
them to make wise decisions
especially to follow christ, I want
to have a foundation to inspire people
to strive for the stars

Battle Lessons
from the Diagnosis

Problems are like washing machines.
They twist us, spin us, knock us around.
But in the end, we come out cleaner, brighter
and better than before.

-Unknown

CHAPTER 7

Those who know me know that I can be both tough and playful. The playfulness probably comes from being forced to grow up fast. I've had too many baptisms by fire experiences. That's why when I get chance to have fun, I take it. The toughness, however, has helped me to survive.

It was one of the most difficult times in my life. I was only thirty-three years old, and at the peak of my career. My first assignment as the pastor of my own church was going well. As a matter of fact, during my tenure at Montclair SDA, I conducted a SWOT analysis, did strategic planning, organized a trip to Israel, did plenty of capital improvements, and fundraised. Attendance increased, membership grew by 84%, and finances grew by a staggering 700%. With barely 250 members, we raised over half a million dollars ($600K) towards the purchase of a building that could accommodate our growth. We were passionate about community and focused a lot on outreach. Accordingly, I sat on several community boards and was fortunate to receive the Carlos Wormley Community Service Award. I was also honored with a joint Legislative Resolution from the Senate and General Assembly of the State of New Jersey for my leadership. It was while I was at Montclair SDA, my life was interrupted with the dreaded diagnosis.

I figured if this was the church where my ministry would end, then I'd had a wonderful ride. Now the question was, "Is this when my life was to end as well?"

I remember walking into the doctor's office because I had discovered a lump during a self-examination. By now I had undergone a lumpectomy and now the results were ready. My husband and I were sitting in the surgeon's office when he walked in. He wasn't a man of many words. He looked calmly at me and said something to the effect of, "I'm sorry, but you have stage three breast cancer." I honestly don't remember his exact words. All I remember is the mental closeup my mind made of his lips as he uttered the word "cancer." I was in complete shock.

I don't remember exactly what I asked next. I think I asked what anyone else in my situation would have. "Am I dying?" I processed his response like a bad cell phone connection. I only remembered hearing key words— "Oh no...spread to lymph nodes...curable stage"—and finally, the words that can make the bravest of us cringe: "chemo." What he said was, I was not going to die. The cancer spread to three lymph nodes, and it's at a curable stage. My oncologist would later tell me, if the cancer had spread to four or more lymph nodes, my case would have been more severe.

By the way, there is a difference between cure and remission. Cure means that there are no traces of your cancer after treatment. Remission means that the signs and symptoms of your cancer are reduced.[13] I was in a curable stage. Nevertheless, I sat there frozen and completely terrified.

The rest of that day is a blur—except for one awesome gesture. I remember walking out of the room and having the nurse at the front desk sit me down on the couch next to her. She then reached into a closet and pulled out a gift bag. It was about 12 x 10 inches large, glossy with a pink and white pattern. It had matching gift bag tissue peeking over the edges, and it was full of goodies.

"What is this?" I asked.

Speaking in a soft voice and tone she said, "This is a gift bag from a local church ministry," she said compassionately. "They provide these to our doctor's office to be given to any patient who has been diagnosed with cancer."

I didn't know which church this was or where it was located. But what timing? After receiving the worst news of my life, this small act from strangers gave me a glimmer of hope. To be honest, I don't remember what the items in the bag were. But as far as I am concerned, the gift bag was filled with love. I paused to swallow in order to reign in my emotions, then said, "Thank you."

I was scheduled to begin treatments in a couple of weeks. I remember wondering "What will it do to my body? Will I look frail like I've seen on TV? How will it impact my daily routine? Only time will tell." My chemo was what they call adjuvant therapy. That meant all tests showed I was cancer-free. Taking chemo was to treat any microscopic cancer cell that might have gone beyond the lymph nodes. The idea is to treat my entire system to remove any possible recurrence down the line.

Ironically, the most difficult part about cancer is not the disease because there is medicine for that. The biggest battle is for your peace of mind. I wish there was a pill to help people manage their reaction to your diagnosis. I'd give it to them in a heartbeat because once they hear the word "cancer," they immediately give you a death sentence. That may be the case for some cancer patients, but not for all of us. We are stigmatized and subjected to constant looks of pity and despair. It does not matter what your test results were, you are labeled as marred. Part of the battle is not letting people's misinformed depression become your own.

One of the major lessons I learned through this experience is not to take battles personally. Life happens, and it happens to everybody. When I was diagnosed with cancer, I was 33 years old. I was married for barely four years. We were still newlyweds when my husband turned into my nurse. Chemo at 33?? Life seemed so unfair. But then I went to my chemo appointment. At the doctor's office, I conversed with the older woman sitting next to me. She looked like she was in her late sixties. I asked her, "Is this your first chemo treatment?" She said, "Oh no, my tumor is too large! I have to do radiation first to shrink it so that I can qualify for chemo." Really? Her words left me speechless. I didn't ask any further questions. I sat in my seat and waited for my name to be called.

When the Oncologist called me in, I didn't know what to expect. I sat in the chair. The nurse started an IV line in my arm. Afterwards, the doctor came in with a bag full of treatment and hooked it up to the IV. I sat until the bag of fluid emptied into my system. I did not feel much until about a day or two later.

The symptoms of chemo can vary. I recall losing my hair, falling out clumps at a time after the first round of treatment. I wasn't fond of how I looked with patches of hair here and there. Since all of it was going to fall out anyway, I asked my husband to shave my head. I remember walking into the bathroom, while facing the mirror, he pulled out his clippers and removed all the hair I had left.

That's a moment I never imagined we would share when we said, "I do." Now, here we were. When he married me, I had a full head of hair. Now it's hair today, gone tomorrow. My head looked like a cue ball. We stared at the mirror together, and he let me evaluate his work. He was so composed it was reassuring. Throughout this experience, my husband created a safe space for me to feel however I wanted to feel, and to look however I wanted to look.

Chemo made all my fingernails and toenails turn black. They gave me a prescription for the nausea, but the pills gave me headaches so vicious I chose to live with the nausea. I would lie for days in the fetal position while the chemo worked its way through my system. My appetite was gone, but it would return just in time for the next round. In that small window when I was hungry and could eat, my husband would get me anything I wanted. Recovering from the first round of chemo, I craved a seven-layer burrito from Taco Bell. My husband dashed out of the house and came back with a couple of burritos and tons of mild sauce. The plastic bag he returned with was bursting with burritos and condiments.

Subsequent surgeries followed, resulting in a temporary inability for me to raise my hands above my head. Clear nails, having an appetite, having hair on any part of your body, the ability to raise your arms, socializing whenever you choose – these are simple things people take for granted. Chemo had radically altered my daily life.

Let's go back to my conversation with the older woman in the doctor's office. She was hoping to qualify for chemo, for my misery. My ordeal was her aspiration! I realized life happens. It happens to the young or old, rich or poor, male or female. Life happens, and it happens to everybody. Don't take it personally.

If you don't like something, change it.
If you can't change it, change the way you think about it.

-Mary Engelbreit

Almost dying can teach you a lot about living. Another lesson I learned was to control your story. To put it another way, the problem I am facing is not always the problem. The real problem is the story I tell myself about the problem.

When you go through a crisis, you can get fixated replaying thoughts such as: "Where did I go wrong?" "I have the worst luck in the world" "I must be paying for something I've done" "I must be a terrible person," "I don't deserve to be happy." The next step is to think, "It's always going to be like this." These thoughts will erode your confidence and feed self-doubt. Thoughts become beliefs. Believing the worst and expecting the worst can hijack the rest of your life sabotaging any attempts at happiness.

I meet people who think what happened to them was because they didn't pray enough. I have to tell them, "It's not because you didn't pray enough." I'm a pastor. I pray more than the average person. I still faced crisis. It's not because you weren't good enough. It's not because there is something inherently wrong with you. Sometimes, things just happen. That's why this next battle-tested lesson is so critical. Control the story you tell yourself.

You determine which thoughts will hold you hostage. Negative thoughts will come. That's inevitable. They don't have to stay. Martin Luther said, "You cannot keep birds from flying over your head, but you can keep them from building a nest in your hair."

On a lighter note, have you noticed people who regularly rehearse negative thoughts like to exaggerate? Every time they tell the story, they add another dismal detail. At first, they say, "I was sick for four months." The next time they tell the story, "I was sick for eight months." They'll say, "After losing my job, I went on three interviews, but no one called me back." The next time they tell the story, "I went on a dozen interviews. I can't get hired because my old boss is out to get me. He called all his friends in the industry spreading lies about me. Now, no one's going to hire me. What's the point?" Do you know people who exaggerate? Here's what can happen. Instead of taking action or moving forward, exaggerating how bad your situation is justifies why you shouldn't do anything to improve it.

Don't exaggerate. Instead disrupt the delusion. If you think bad things are always happening to you, make a list of the good things that have happened to you as well. Pessimistic people tend to overreact to adversity. Therefore, having the facts on your side is a powerful tool for disrupting the delusion of catastrophe created in the pessimistic mind. After making your new list, challenge your original thought with the truth generated by the evidence. "Some bad things happen to me, but plenty of good things happen to me as well." You may also try writing down three to five positive things that happened to you during the day every night for at least a week. Hopefully, these exercises will help free you from ruminating on negative thoughts.

My husband, Smith, is also a pastor. Our favorite part of the job is visitation, for one visit can make a big difference. It may sound like I am referring to the one being visited. Actually, the greatest impact often happens to the one doing the visiting.

I remember Smith coming home from a hospital visit. I could tell something happened that affected him. I asked him if he'd like to talk about it. He told me about the lady he went to see. She was a senior citizen. We'll call her Mary. Unlike others he'd visited that week, she was a double amputee. When Mary was in her forties, she developed diabetes. Eventually, she had both legs removed. Bedridden and in the hospital, she was always the happiest person he'd see. She would talk about God's goodness and how grateful she was. That day when he visited, he found that one of her hands had also been amputated. What struck him was, she had one hand and no legs, but she was still beaming. He described her as radiant. They chatted for a while then he sang and prayed with her.

In short, Smith was moved by her tenacity of spirit. Henry David Thoreau said, "It's not what you look at that matters, but what you see." I think that was true for Mary. She refused to have negative thoughts hold her hostage. What people saw when they looked at her was different from what she saw in herself. She had life. She had family. She had her right mind, and she had an unshakeable relationship with God. She took control of her story, so can we.

Application Exercises

1. Who have been some of the most supportive people in your life?

   Lorena, Albert, Smarisel, Cleo
   Vivian, Lourdes

2. List some of the significant issues people around you have dealt with or are dealing with right now. How did you assist them?

   Divorce/separation - Encouragement drving
   owe water, My sisters (house)

3. List some of your positive experiences.

   — Summit
   — Buying a House
   — good paying Job

True friends aren't the ones who make your problems disappear. They're the ones who won't disappear when you're facing problems.

-Unknown

Battle Lessons from the Inner Circle

CHAPTER 8

Sometimes, I think my husband's a little crazy. In the middle of my chemo treatments, he approached me and said, "I think it's time for you to get your doctorate." I remember thinking to myself, "What in the world is going through his mind?! What is it about my condition that even hints that I can take on another challenge?" I replied, "What?" Without flinching, he repeated himself. You have to understand something about my husband. He is a natural introvert. That means he thinks about what he is going to say a thousand times before actually saying it. He's looked at all the factors, considered all the options, and contemplated the pitfalls and benefits. Then he speaks. You must be on your A-game to get him to change his mind. Clearly, I wasn't.

I said, "I still have a couple of more treatments."

"You can study and write in between treatments," he said undeterred.

"In a few months, I will be back at work fulltime," I argued.

"It's a distance learning program," he answered. "We would only have to travel a couple of times a year for the intensives."

"What if I don't feel strong enough to travel?" I asked apprehensively.

"The travel dates do not conflict with your chemo schedule," he responded. "I'll travel with you. We'll do this together."

That was it. Trying to talk him out of it was futile. A few weeks later, we both enrolled in the Doctor of Ministry program at United Theological Seminary. I finished the program in two and a half years. My husband took slightly longer. It was not because he was failing classes. He's an honor student. However, at the time, he was pastoring three churches. I had only one. The demand on his time became a challenge. As a result, he put his education on pause for a semester and focused on helping me finish my degree. After I completed the program, I did not participate in my summer graduation ceremony. I received permission from the dean to walk instead in my husband's graduation scheduled for the Winter. Smith resumed his studies, then in December 2012, we walked across the stage together. We got hooded together. We received our diplomas together.

Be willing to be a beginner every single morning.

-Meister Eckhart

Adversity can destroy you or it can be an opportunity to reinvent yourself. Studies show that being able to reinvent yourself is a common quality in successful leaders, executives, and athletes. Competitors and opponents use your past success as a blueprint to strategize against. Continually honing your skills and developing new skills helps you to stay ahead of the pack.

I remember the story about a twelve-year-old boy who decided to study judo, although he had lost his left arm in a devastating car accident. The boy began lessons with an old Japanese judo master. The boy was doing well, so he couldn't understand why, after three months of training, the master had taught him only one move.

"Sensei," the boy finally said, "Shouldn't I be learning more moves?"

"This is the only move you know, but this is the only move you'll ever need to know," the sensei replied.

Not quite understanding, but believing in his teacher, the boy kept training. Several months later, the sensei took the boy to his first tournament. Surprising himself, the boy easily won his first two matches. The third match proved to be more difficult, but after some time, his opponent became impatient and charged—the boy deftly used his one move to win the match. Still amazed by his success, the boy was now in the finals. This time, his opponent was bigger, stronger, and more experienced.

For a while, the boy appeared to be overmatched. Concerned that the boy might get hurt, the referee called a time-out. He was about to stop the match when the sensei intervened. "No," the sensei insisted, "let him continue."

Soon after the match resumed, his opponent made a critical mistake: he dropped his guard. Instantly, the boy used his move to pin him. The boy had won the match and the tournament. He was the champion.

On the way home, the boy and sensei reviewed every move in every single match. Then the boy summoned the courage to ask what was really on his mind. "Sensei, how did I win the tournament with only one move?"

"You won for two reasons," the sensei answered. "First, you've almost mastered one of the most difficult throws in all of judo. And second, the only known defense for that move is for your opponent to grip your left arm."

Whatever adversity took from you can turn into an advantage. Explore new possibilities, level up your skills. In this way, when crisis forces a change, your transformation becomes an upgrade.

> *If life keeps knocking you down, find a way to fall on your back.*
> *If you fall on your back, you can look up.*
> *If you can look up, you can get up.*

-Les Brown

The story of Play-Doh began when Kutol, a Cincinnati-based soap company, was about to go out of business. Children love to play with it. However, it was not originally used for fun and games but for cleaning.

Before World War II, coal was the typical way people heated their homes, and it would leave soot stains on the walls. Noah and Joseph McVicker of Kutol Products created the dough-like material to rub the soot off wallpaper. The product kept the business afloat for over a decade. Then came a change. After the war, natural gas became a more common heat source. Coal was being phased out. The McVickers had plenty of supply, but demand plummeted, and the company was facing bankruptcy.

Kay Zufall, the sister-in law of Joseph McVicker, came to the rescue. As a schoolteacher, she used the material in her classroom as modeling dough. The kids had so much fun Kay called Joe and suggested a new purpose for their product. That is how Play-Doh was born. The McVickers removed the detergent from the material and marketed their product as a children's toy. They sold it to schools all throughout Cincinnati. Not long afterwards, Joe secured the endorsement of Captain Kangaroo, and sales skyrocketed.

Play-Doh was sold in 1956 at Woodward and Lothrop, a department store in Washington, D.C. Initially, it came in only one color—off-white. Colored Play-Doh came out the following year and was sold at Macy's in New York and other department stores. Needless to say, the McVickers became millionaires.

To summarize, after the war, the McVickers faced bankruptcy. Their product seemed worthless. But then a component was removed from the material, and a new substance was born. The McVickers became millionaires because of that change. When tragedy strikes, it leaves you changed. You may not be who you used to be, but you never lost your value. Reinvent yourself and you'll discover you're priceless.

*You're the average of the five people
you spend most of your time with.*

-Jim Rohn

I am not sure how Rohn came up with the number five, but I know the McVickers were glad Kay was in that number. Research does confirm that our friends affect our personal growth: "...it has become increasingly clear that our peers are stealth sculptors of everything from our basic linguistic habits to our highest aspirations."[14]

Every once in a while, reinventing yourself means reinventing your inner circle. Why not perform a friendship detox by taking inventory of the company you keep. You need friends who will partner with you in the belief that you can be better, and you can do better. Seek out the company of those who will stretch you. "...if you befriend those who are already accomplishing what you've been independently struggling to achieve, your habits will more easily converge with theirs."[15]

Some of us don't have friends. We have enablers. An enabler is not a friend. Someone who supports your bad habits or makes it easier for you to continue damaging behavior is not a friend. That is one type of enabler. There is a second type of enabler. The first type encourages you towards a destructive path. The second ignores your self-destructive behavior. This enabler is someone who just wants to avoid conflict, and their desire to avoid conflicts with you is greater than their desire for you to be a better you. Instead, quality inner circle friends help you see the bigger picture when you are tempted to make bad choices. When you are angry, they remind you not to make a permanent decision on temporary emotions. When you are tempted to experiment with something addictive, they remind you it's easier not to start a habit than to break a habit. Good friends would rather see you bruised than ruined. I love the way it's stated in Prov. 27:6, "Wounds from a friend can be trusted, but an enemy multiplies kisses."

The best inner circle consists of people who sympathize when you share bad news, and they know how to lean in when you share good news. What do I mean by leaning in? When a person shares good news, there are generally three ways the listener can respond. They can lean back, just lean, or lean in. If you say, "My application has been approved. I am ready to start my own business!" Those who lean back would say, "Why'd you do that? What bank in their right mind will give you a loan? Even if you do find one crazy enough to approve your loan, most businesses nowadays fail in the first few months. You're going to be in a lot of debt." If they don't ignore the good news and change the subject, they immediately offer negative feedback. The person who just leans would say," Oh, nice" and offer no further commentary. They do not tear down the idea, but neither are they enthusiastic about it. The person who leans in would say, "That's fantastic! How did it feel when you received the letter in the mail?" Those who lean in respond with a level of zeal. Furthermore, they ask questions to help you almost re-experience the moment. Inner circle friends are a precious commodity. Choose them wisely.

An African proverb teaches, "If you want to go fast, go alone. If you want to go far, go together." Yes, I thought Smith had gone a little crazy that day. Yet, we climbed the mountain together. I thank God for him. I couldn't have asked for a better companion."

Application Exercises

1. What are the characteristics of the five people you spend the most time with?

A._____

_____

_____

B._____

_____

_____

C._____

_____

_____

_____

D._____

_____

_____

E._____

_____

_____

_____

2. Identify two areas of interest you would like to explore.
   Interview people who are proficient in those fields.

A._____

_____

_____

B._____

_____

_____

3. What did you learn from the interviews?

_____

_____

_____

_____

_____

_____

_____

_____

_____

_____

_____

_____

Battle Lessons from the Body and Mind

Worry is a thin stream of fear trickling through the mind.
If encouraged, it cuts a channel into which
all other thoughts are drained.

-Arthur S. Roche

CHAPTER 9

Fighting cancer is a battle for the mind for a couple of reasons. The first was mentioned earlier. I had to resist internalizing the sadness of the misinformed people I encountered.

Another reason for the mental battle is because cancer is often asymptomatic, which means symptoms are not always apparent. Because you can become sick and walk around without symptoms, you start to think everything is a symptom: a new itch, a slight pain here, another one there. In between checkups, worry can dominate your thoughts.

Early in my treatment, my oncologist would prescribe periodic nuclear scans to identify cancer activity anywhere in my body. They would find a vein that hadn't been damaged by chemo and inject radioactive material. Then I'd wait for the scan. The results of every scan came back clear, and I realized I had wasted precious time worrying over nothing. The itch was just an itch.

In between checkups, I learned to live my life with fulness as well as prudence. From day one, I began juicing. The recipes were various combinations of vegetables—carrots, kale, spinach, etc.—and sweetened with fruits. Carrot juice was my favorite and still is. Doesn't that sound delicious? It can be. I'm not recommending you become a health fanatic. However, you should be a fan of your health. Everyone should be health conscious. Developing cancer is a life-altering experience. Nevertheless, it does not mean the person has met his or her quota for developing disease. It's not the only malady that can affect you. As a rule, try to do what's best for your body to give yourself every advantage possible to fight any sickness.

Healthy habits should be promoted alongside healthy diets. I think habit formation is where the real struggle is for most people. Here are some lessons to keep in mind:

You do not rise to the level of your goals.
You fall to the level of your systems.

-James Clear

Whether we know it or not, all of us have developed systems. Some systems are by design, others by default. The behaviors we engage in by default are what I call habits. Excessive drinking, smoking, and drug addiction are the habitual behaviors that people typically think of when discussing bad habits. Of course, we should be cognizant of their destructive influence. However, we should also be mindful of hindering habits. These are the little practices that obstruct our progress and sabotage our goals. Hindering habits hide in our daily routines.

My most successful lifestyle changes have started with journaling, when I took the time to write down everything I did during the day. Try it. You'll be surprised what you discover as you read over your entries. In a short period of time, I began to implement changes. Journaling worked for at least two reasons. Reading my daily entries helped me hold myself accountable. I wanted to have a good record to reflect on at the end of the day. That was only going to happen if I did things I could be proud of. I wanted to see that I completed tasks, finished my to-do list, and was helpful to others. Second, journaling brought about awareness. I noticed I hadn't been paying attention to some counter-productive practices. By becoming aware of them, I could make a change.

Until you make the unconscious conscious, it will direct your life,
and you will call it fate.

-Carl G. Jung

Habit formation is incredibly useful because the conscious mind is the bottleneck of the brain. It can only pay attention to one problem at a time. As a result, your brain is always working to preserve your conscious attention for whatever task is most essential. Whenever possible, the conscious mind likes to pawn off tasks to the nonconscious mind to do automatically. This is precisely what happens when a habit is formed.[16]

We are wired to develop habits. It's the brain's way of conserving cognitive energy and allows us to multitask. For example, the route to work is so familiar, you can make turns, press the gas, hit the brakes, check your mirrors, change lanes all while listening to your latest audio book. Because you travel this route as frequently as you do your brain shifts into autopilot allowing you to process new information while driving.

Studies show that much of our behavior is determined by elements in our environment that operate outside of conscious awareness.[17] That means sometimes going into autopilot is preceded by a trigger. This is possible because we process some information consciously, and others subconsciously. Industries, including restaurants, retail and supermarkets, use this knowledge to their advantage. For example, color is an emotional cue. Different colors evoke different emotions. Red is associated with excitement, passion, and danger. It's an attention grabber. One UC Berkley study showed people are attracted to colors associated with objects to which they have positive reactions.[18] Consider the color of the sky or clear waters. Most people are unlikely to have a negative association with the color blue. This is probably why blue is so popular. Think of Facebook, LinkedIn, Skype, Intel, Dell, and Walmart. Blue induces feelings of calm, serenity, loyalty, and trust. Other studies show each industry has their preference. Black is the color of sophistication. It is considered to be the height of elegance in the retail world.[19]

Colors are one cue—product placement is another. Restaurant menu layouts influence meal selection. Experts in menu design claim the upper-right side of the menu is a "sweet spot." Items listed there are purchased with more frequency.[20]

The same concept applies to product placement in grocery stores. Have you noticed where milk is usually placed? As a popular perishable item, milk is placed in the back of the store to encourage shoppers to travel around the entire store. Manufacturers pay retailers slotting allowances, which are payments to secure specific shelf space, because customers are more likely to purchase items placed at eye level or in the end of the aisle displays. On account of their placement, end of aisle displays make up 30-40% of all supermarket sales. Now, what about items at the checkout register? We can't forget those. This is a popular point-of-sale area where retailers place impulse buy items such as magazines, candy, gum, soft drinks, and other sweets.[21]

Retailers develop cues for all five senses. However, the majority of triggers cater to the sense of sight. Some consider sight the most relied upon and important sense for most humans.[22] French academic Frédéric Brochet conducted an experiment that underscores the power of the sense of sight. You may have heard of the field of Enology. It is the study of wine. Brochet conducted a wine comparison test with fifty-four undergraduates from the Faculty of Oenology of the University of Bordeaux. These were trained wine-tasters. Twenty-seven male and twenty-seven female oenology students were given a glass of red and a glass of white wine. He asked them to describe the flavor of each. The students described the white with terms like "honey," "lemon," "grapefruit," and "banana." The red wine was described with words such as "chicory," "coal," "clove," and "cherry."

The students were invited back a week later for another tasting. Again, Brochet offered them a glass of red wine and a glass of white, but this time he added a twist. The two wines were actually the same white wine as before, but he dyed one with tasteless red food coloring. With only the visual sense altered, what would be the result? Surprisingly, these wine connoisseurs described the white wine dyed red with the same vocabulary commonly ascribed to red wine. In other words, without knowing it, they used red-wine language to describe white wine in disguise. Because of what they saw, the tasters discounted information from their sense of taste and smell.

What you allow yourself to see is not without consequences. Consider using that as leverage to break hindering habits and establish helpful ones. Do you want to curb your spending habits? Instead of grabbing what's at eye-level at the store, stoop down. There are less expensive items that may be of the same or comparable quality stored on the lower shelves. Another helpful practice is to remove items associated with your negative habits from your view. If you have trouble focusing, study in a room without the television. Put your mobile phone in another room until your task is complete. That way, you won't be distracted by calls and notifications. If you easily fall prey to sweets, take the cookie jar out of your line of sight. Place it in the cupboard you frequent the least. Instead, place some fruit or some other healthy snack you enjoy where the cookies used to be.

Use your vision to motivate yourself. Create vision boards with pictures of what you want to accomplish. Hang your sneakers on the doorknob on your bedroom door, the bathroom door, or the front door to remind you to exercise. Try writing out a to-do list and post it on your bedroom mirror.

We've learned you can have long-term change by forming helpful habits. Habit formation is influenced by managing our environment, putting your subconscious to work for you and not against you. Let's now address what can be done on the conscious level to affect behavior change.

First, be consistent—whether in public or in private.

If you are persistent, you will get it.
If you are consistent, you will keep it.

-Unknown

I must confess. I am not a New England Patriots fan. If you are, that's fine, but before you get upset, let me tell you my side of the story. My dad introduced me to the NFL, and he was a diehard Dolphins fan. We would watch Dan Marino—the greatest quarterback without a Super Bowl ring—and the Miami Dolphins play every Sunday. And in elementary school, they taught us the Miami Dolphins fight song. The chorus was simple but catchy: "Miami Dolphins, Miami Dolphins, Miami Dolphins number one." As a consequence, I was well indoctrinated. I grew up during a time when the Dolphins-Patriots rivalry was alive and well, and till this day, I still harbor some rather strong feelings against the Patriots. Did someone say, "Deflategate?"

Despite my animus towards the organization, their success is undeniable and instructive. I watched the September 23, 2001 game when the Jets linebacker Mo Lewis leveled a heavy hit on the Patriots quarterback. Just like that, Drew Bledsoe was replaced by the Patriots backup quarterback Tom Brady. The Patriots never looked back. Brady was the 199th overall draft pick, yet he's arguably the most accomplished quarterback in the history of the sport. He has nine Superbowl appearances, six Superbowl rings, and is a four-time Superbowl MVP. He has orchestrated some of the most amazing comebacks in the regular season and the Superbowl.

In a video interview, Brady was asked his thoughts on replacing Drew Bledsoe. He stated,

If I was in that situation, I wouldn't know how I could have dealt with it. When you're the quarterback, you always feel like I've had a big part to do with this game. When you're the backup quarterback, you don't even feel like you're on a team. You feel like you're a fan. You know, like I didn't do anything to help our team win. You always feel that, I'm just taking up space.[23]

In Brady's seasons as a backup, he felt like he was just taking up space. Impressively, in spite of feeling this way about his role, he stayed game-ready. When Coach Belichick put him in the game, his work-ethic was on display for all to see. His consistency off the field in his backup role helped him excel in the starting position. Consistency matters.

Success isn't always about greatness. It's about consistency.
Consistent hard work leads to success. Greatness will come.

-Dwayne Johnson

Second, minor changes can lead to major results.

Too often, we convince ourselves that massive success requires massive action. Whether it is losing weight, building a business, writing a book, winning a championship, or achieving any other goal, we put pressure on ourselves to make some earth-shattering improvement that everyone will talk about.[24]

If you think you must pull off a single remarkable act to achieve your goal, you may keep putting it off. Usually, what it takes to get you to your goal is a series of small, achievable steps repeated again and again. Remember, results are the product of routine. It's wonderful that you have a goal. Congratulations! Once you set that goal, the lion's share of your energy and willpower should be focused on maintaining the routine that will get you there. Consistency is king. According to a 2005 study by ThinkTQ, only 7 percent of people take action daily toward the attainment of at least one goal.[25] If you can be consistent with at least one practice toward your goals, you will be in rare company.

Perhaps you are eager to achieve a certain look, a certain income, or be promoted to a certain position. If you focus more on the end result instead of the routine, you may become frustrated that you are so far from your destination. Success is usually a delayed reaction to your routines. You may not notice any changes at first. However, your daily practices are working like water against the cracks in a dam. Eventually, there will be a breakthrough with undeniable results.

Don't wait till you reach your goal to be proud of yourself. Be proud of every step you take towards reaching your goal.

-Unknown

Third, be patient with yourself. Are you trying to make a long-overdue change? Chances are, you didn't get in your current condition overnight. If that is the case, then you're probably like most people. Change will not happen overnight either.

Impatience will decimate your progress. If the breakthrough takes too long in your estimation, you may fall back on unhealthy coping mechanisms that will undo all you've accomplished. You may return to stress-eating, blaming others for your situation, or succumb to defeatist thinking and say, "What's the point?" It's better for everyone if you are patient with yourself.

As a matter of fact, no matter how strong our willpower, we're virtually guaranteed to fall occasionally back into our old ways. Don't get alarmed, relapses are part of long-term habit change. We must plan for those setbacks so that we do not throw in the towel.

Smokers often quit and then start smoking again as many as seven times before giving up cigarettes for good. Research by James Prochaska at the University of Rhode Island and others shows that as smokers quit, and then relapse, they begin to achieve a self-awareness about the cues and rewards that drive their smoking patterns. The first few times we fail to change, we're probably not aware why. However, as a pattern emerges— "I'm usually good at resisting in the afternoon, but it's the mornings when I really struggle"—we start to understand, and analyze what's really going on. "We learn about ourselves sometimes without knowing we're learning... That's why failure is so valuable. It forces us to learn, even if we don't want to."[26]

You know the old adage, "Every setback is a setup for a comeback."

Look for three things in a person—intelligence, energy and integrity.
If they don't have the last one, don't even bother with the first two.

-Warren Buffet

There is one more aspect to consistency we need to consider. It's the aspect of consistency that overlaps with integrity. Studies have shown individuals have an innate desire to be viewed as being consistent. Their beliefs must match their actions, especially when they take a public stand.

One such study was conducted by consumer researcher Daniel Howard in Dallas, TX. Individuals were called and asked to contribute to a charitable cause. Whenever someone picked up the phone, one set of callers rushed to ask, "We are raising funds for...Would you like to help us out by..." The request was always for a worthy cause. Another group of callers would first ask, "How are you doing today?" or "How are you feeling today?" Then they would pause and wait for a response. People would commonly respond with a polite, "Just fine," "Good," or "I'm doing great. Thanks." After eliciting a response, the caller would then make their pitch. Which group do you think raised the most funds? The first group achieved 18% agreement. 32% of those called by the second group agreed to participate. In the end, the latter group raised more money.[27]

Once the person acknowledged out loud all is well, it became easier to convince the person to help those who were not doing well. "I'm glad to hear that, because I'm calling to ask if you'd be willing to make a donation to help out the unfortunate victims of..." Not to help would seem awkward or even selfish. If you believe you are a good person, you are motivated to do what a good person should do in that situation.

Put this principle to work for you. Make your goals or new commitments public by communicating them to a trusted friend or friends. They can hold you accountable, and you will naturally be driven to act in ways consistent with a stand you have taken publicly.

In summary, you can improve your quality of life by taking care of your mind and body. We all have formed habits if properly managed can yield significant positive results. Redesign your environment to encourage an alternate course of action, putting your subconscious to work for you. Being consistent will improve your performance and help you maintain the rewards you've earned. And, don't forget, results are the product of routine. If you want better results, change your routine. That may not always be easy. Notwithstanding, life will only change when you are more committed to your dreams than you are to your comfort zone.

Application Exercises

1. Track your behavior for the next 24 hours and record it below. Review the record at the end of the day and identify what was positive, neutral, and negative behavior.

_____

_____

_____

_____

_____

2. What are some changes you would like to make in your life? Break them down into smaller steps.

_____

_____

_____

_____

_____

3. Who are you going to share your commitment(s) with?

_____

_____

_____

_____

_____

Battle Lessons from Survival

Cancer is a word, not a sentence.

-John Diamond

CHAPTER 10

I am currently celebrating 10 years being cancer-free! That means it has been at least 120 months, 3650 days, 87,600 hours, 5,259,492 minutes, 315,569,520 seconds of living beyond the interruption. Celebrating milestones in the workplace promotes a positive environment, incentivizes people to reach goals, and reinforces the behavior that helped realize the accomplishment. Milestones related to sickness, on the other hand, remind you to appreciate life and to make the most of every moment. When you've been blessed with a second chance at living, do not squander it.

The crucible is where champions are made. Once you've stood up to cancer, you sort of pity all other opponents. As a leader, occasionally, people will challenge you for the sake of challenging you. When that happens to me, I look at them and think, "But you're not chemo. I've had to face down harsh realities and confront my own mortality. What makes you think you can intimidate me? I'm built for battle." I've developed an even greater boldness, and I'm not the only one. Listen to these celebrity women:

If it weren't for my breast cancer, I wouldn't be a 'Today' host.
After I got better, I talked to my boss about working on the show.
Six months before, I'd have been terrified to go in there and ask
for what I wanted. But after what I'd been through, how could I be
scared of being told no?

-Hoda Kotb

I laughed more in the hospital than I ever have in my life,
making fun of all the weird things that were happening to me.
My friends would walk in with this sad look,
and I would throw something at them and say,
'Come on! This isn't the end of the world!'

-Christina Applegate

I do not feel any less of a woman.
I feel empowered that I made a strong choice
that in no way diminishes my femininity.

-Angelina Jolie

Fight each round, take it on the chin.
And never never never ever give in.

Olivia Newton John in her song "Why Me,"
a tribute to her battle with breast cancer.

You may not have had to fight cancer at 33 years old, but I bet you've had to fight. No one escapes suffering, fear, and pain. In life, you have to expect the unexpected, no matter how well you plan. So how do you go through hardships and come out on the other side? How do you move through heartache to happiness or from suffering to strength? Some call it hardiness. Others call it resilience. Whichever you choose to call it, the principles are the same.

The first principle of resilience is, don't resist reality. What you resist persists and sometimes grows. Accept your life for what it is, even if it means dealing with negative experiences and emotions. Processing regrets and disappointments may cause you to cry. In those moments, think of the words of author Matshona Dhliwayo, "Tears are the sweat of champions." Give yourself credit for being courageous enough to take the journey. It will pay dividends, because decisions based on reality are less likely to crumble when faced with adversity.

Second, resilient people have positive core values. Core values are fundamental beliefs that direct our thoughts and behavior. They help us determine what is important. Our definitions of success and failure are based on our values. Accordingly, values also help us interpret our experiences.

Third, they are innovative. Resilient people have a knack for imagining possibilities. Although an object may have been designed for a specific purpose, they can see other possibilities for its use. I think of my favorite posts on Facebook—home hacks. It's when people take ordinary household products and devise new uses for them. For example, shaving cream meant for aiding in hair removal is used as a cleaning product. It can clean carpets and stainless steel. Coat hangers meant for hanging clothes can be fashioned into a portable shelf for hanging books. Having trouble threading a needle? Spritz hairspray on the end of the thread to stiffen it. Now, it will be easier to guide it through the eye of the needle. Resilient people do the same with life. Their ability to imagine possibilities is one reason they can manage harsh realities.

Fourth, resilient people do more than bounce back. Their disposition is akin to the quote, "Throw me to the wolves and I'll return leading the pack." Not only can they adapt, but they also have the capacity to improve.

If you are going through an awful ordeal, take an action that creates excitement about the future. When my husband enrolled us in a doctoral program while I was still undergoing chemo treatments, he kindled in me an excitement about my future.

Your present circumstances don't determine where you can go,
they merely determine where you start.

-Nido Qubein

What about you? Are you getting the most out of life? Are you reaching your full potential? Or are you still having a pity party about your issues? Are you caught in the aftershocks of an unexpected crisis and having difficulty moving forward? I've been there. But remember, "We do not heal the past by dwelling there, we heal the past by living fully in the present."

It turns out the crisis gave me an opportunity, not just to go through it, but to grow through it. On the 2nd anniversary of completing chemotherapy, I successfully passed my doctoral defense. I walked out of the room as Dr. Paula Olivier. I joined the John Maxwell Team and became a certified speaker, trainer, and coach. I became the first female pastor of Haitian heritage in my denomination—credentialed and with a DMin. My father was rather proud of that achievement. I've traveled the world sharing my testimony encouraging others with and without cancer. I've seen lives changed.

One of the most difficult parts of my diagnosis was seeing the look on the faces of my doctors, nurses, and other medical professionals. Whenever they viewed my chart or learned why I was being seen, a look of hurt and sadness came over their faces. They would often see me and say, "But you're so young?" I was one of the youngest women they've had to treat for breast cancer. But guess what? That is not the only time I've been the youngest in the room.

Going back to work meant resuming my meetings with community leaders. As a pastor, I maintain relationships with our civic leaders, which includes mayors, senators, and city council members. When I returned to those meetings, I was the youngest in the room with a doctorate. I sat on boards of community coalitions, again, I was the youngest in the room invited to the table. My members were proud. My youthfulness was not a reason for pity. To those around me and to thousands I've had a chance to speak to, I became an inspiration—a trailblazer.

Since cancer, I have traveled the world. I have climbed up the leaning tower of Pisa, climbed down the Eiffel Tower, walked through the Roman Colosseum, sand-boarded in the Arabian Desert, and sailed on the Sea of Galilee to name a few. Cancer is indeed a word, not a sentence.

You may be wondering, "Are resilient people born or made?" Can resiliency be taught? Studies show, without question, it can be taught. Virtually, anyone can learn resilience. That is great news because battles are coming. That's life. When they do, remember some of the lessons shared in this book. Don't take it personally. Control the story you tell yourself about your struggles. Failure is never final. Reinvent yourself. Take on a challenge. Face harsh realities, develop core values, imagine possibilities, and you will bounce back stronger than ever. Take it from a battle-tested life. Your story is just beginning.

Application Exercises

1.   What crucibles have you emerged from?

_____

_____

_____

_____

_____

_____

2.   What did they teach you?

_____

_____

_____

_____

_____

_____

3.   Who do you know that can benefit from your story?

_____

_____

_____

_____

_____

_____

Appendix

Endnotes

1. J Maxwell, John C... *Today Matters: 12 Daily Practices to Guarantee Tomorrow's Success* (Maxwell, John C.) (p. 3). Center Street. Kindle Edition.
2. Linkagoal (published October 14, 2015) *Research Reveals Fear of Failure Has Us All Shaking in Our Boots This Halloween* https://www.globenewswire.com/news-release/2015/10/14/1060928/0/en/Research-Reveals-Fear-of-Failure-Has-Us-All-Shaking-in-Our-Boots-This-Halloween.html (accessed 11/1/19)
3. *The Business Journals* (published December 3, 2014) 7 revealing quotes from Amazon chief Jeff Bezos on failures, Fire, books and more https://www.bizjournals.com/bizjournals/news/2014/12/03/7-quotes-from-amazon-jeff-bezos-on-failure-more.html (accessed 11/1/19)
4. Silicon Valley Historical Association (published October 31, 2011) https://www.youtube.com/watch?v=zkTf0LmDqKl (accessed 11/1/19)
5. Hewlett, Sylvia Ann. *Executive Presence* (pp. 5-6). HarperBusiness. Kindle Edition.
6. Lauren Landry, *Why Emotional Intelligence is Important in Leadership*, Harvard Business Review, April 3, 2019 https://online.hbs.edu/blog/post/emotional-intelligence-in-leadership
7. Gilovich, Thomas, Medvec, Victoria Husted. The temporal pattern to the experience of regret, *Journal of Personality and Social Psychology*, Vol 67(3), Sep 1994, 357-365
8. Adam Kloppe, (2015, March 5), *The Louisiana Purchase and the Haitian Revolution*, Missouri Historical Society. Retrieve from http://mohistory.org/blog/the-louisiana-purchase-and-the-haitian-revolution/ Laurent Dubois & John D. Garrigus (2017) *Slave Revolution in the Caribbean, 1789- 1804: A Brief History with Documents*, 2nd Ed. Bedford Series in History and Cultura) (Kindle Locations 957-958).
9. *The Impact of the Revolution.* Alexandre Pétion. The Schomburg Center for Research in Black Culture: The Abolition of the Slave Trade. New York Public Library Retrieved November 3, 2019 from http://abolition.nypl.org/images/african_resistance/6/29
10. Ada Ferrer, (Feb 2012), *Haiti, Free Soil, and Antislavery in the Revolutionary Atlantic*. American Historical Review, 117(1), 40-66. Pg. 57.
11. Mandela, Nelson. *Long Walk to Freedom* (p. 95). Little, Brown and Company. Kindle Edition.

12. Mandela, Nelson. *The Prison Letters of Nelson Mandela* (p. 81). Liveright. Kindle Edition.
13. https://www.cancer.gov/about-cancer/diagnosis-staging/prognosis#cure-remission-difference
14. Flora, Carlin. *Friendfluence* (p. 2). Knopf Doubleday Publishing Group. Kindle Edition.
15. Flora, p. 236
16. Clear, James. *Atomic Habits* (p. 46). Penguin Publishing Group. Kindle Edition.
17. D. A. Cohen and S. H. Babey, "Contextual Influences on Eating Behaviours: Heuristic Processing and Dietary Choices," *Obesity Reviews* 13, no. 9 (2012), doi:10.1111/j.1467–789x.2012.01001.
18. Stephen E. Palmer and Karen B. Schloss, *An ecological valence theory of human color preference*, PNAS May 11, 2010 107 (19) 8877-8882, https://doi.org/10.1073/pnas.0906172107
19. https://digitalsynopsis.com/design/logo-colour-branding-psychology-industry-specific/
20. D. A. Cohen and S. H. Babey, "Contextual Influences on Eating Behaviours: Heuristic Processing and Dietary Choices," *Obesity Reviews* 13, no. 9 (2012), doi:10.1111/j.1467–789x.2012.01001.
21. Ibid.
22. Rupini RV & Nandagopal R. (2015). *A Study on the Influence of Senses and the Effectiveness of Sensory Branding*, Journal of Psychiatry, 18 (2). Pg. 3. Retrieved from https://www.longdom.org/open-access/a-study-on-the-influence-of- senses-and-the-effectiveness-of-sensorybranding-Psychiatry-1000236.pdf
23. https://www.youtube.com/watch?v=yGnD-2zUidM
24. Clear, James. *Atomic Habits* (p. 15). Penguin Publishing Group. Kindle Edition
25. John C. Maxwell, *Put Your Dreams to the Test*, Thomas Nelson: Nashville, 2009. pg.75
26. Duhigg, Charles. *The Power of Habit: Why We Do What We Do in Life and Business*. Random House Publishing Group. Kindle Edition.
27. Cialdini PhD, Robert B. *Influence* (Collins Business Essentials) (p. 68). HarperCollins e-books. Kindle Edition.

Chasseurs-Volontaires de Saint-Domingue:

Free Soldiers of Color from Haiti

Daniel Fils-Aimé, Sr. & The Haitian-American Historical
Society (HAHS) were responsible for the erection
of the Chasseurs-Voluntaires de Saint-Domingue monument.
The monument is in Savannah's Jefferson Square
and commemorates the free Haitian men
who died battling on behalf of U.S. independence.
Fils-Aimé was both the chairman and founder of HAHS.

Sympathy Resolution

The Honorable Frederica S. Wilson
United States House of Representatives
24ᵗʰ District, Florida

Mr. Speaker, I, Congresswoman Frederica S. Wilson, from the 24th district of the great state of Florida, seek recognition. I rise today to commemorate the life and legacy of an incredible community leader, husband, father and friend – Daniel Fils-Aimé, Sr.

Whereas, Daniel Fils-Aimé was born in Haiti. After successfully completing high school in Port-au-Prince, he migrated to Montreal, Canada, Brooklyn, New York, and Miami, Florida to continue his studies. Prior to beginning his community-based work, Mr. Fils-Aimé studied Mechanical and Technical Diesel, Diesel Mechanics, Realty and Appraisal, and Ground Transportation Specialty Surface Transit and Rail; and

Whereas, Daniel Fils-Aimé is the founder and chairman of the Haitian American Historical Society (HAHS) established in 2001. HAHS is dedicated to educating and promoting Haitian history through art and cultural events for a better understanding of the rich history and positive cooperation between Haitians, Haitian-Americans and other cultures. Under his leadership, the organization was able to commemorate the efforts of the Haitian soldiers that fought for America's independence by building a monument in Savannah, Georgia; and

Whereas, Daniel Fils-Aimé has provided for his community by founding the ground transportation service Miami Mini Bus. The service has transported the residents of Miami-Dade County for over twenty years.; and

Whereas, Daniel Fils-Aimé is not only held in high regard in the Haitian community, he is also admired in various sectors including corporate, political and the arts. His humility and trustworthiness has led him to found and be a board member of various organizations; and

Whereas, Daniel Fils-Aimé is survived by his wife and life partner, Eugenie Fils-Aimé (born Eugenie Davilmar); five children, Dr. Marcelle Tharmarajah (born Fils-Aimé) and husband Sashi, Daniel Fils-Aimé, Jr. and wife, Carole, Nonese Kissane (born Fils-Aimé) and husband Patrick, Dr. Paula Olivier (born Fils-Aimé) and husband Smith, Ashley Fils-Aimé and wife Amani; Five grand-children, Sashi Tharmarajah, Adrian Tharmarajah, Jolianne Jones, Jayden Jones, Kayah Jones; Step-Mother, Romania Fils-Aimé, Brothers: Samuel Fils-Aimé, Emmanuel Fils-Aimé, Isaac Fils-Aimé, Jacques Fils-Aimé Sisters: Mimose Sylvain (born Fils-Aimé), Marie-Altagrace Deshommes, Marie-Micaelle Leroy (born Fils-Aimé), Acefie Amedee (born Fils-Aimé), Jacline Deshomme, along with the many nephews and nieces. He will be greatly missed in South Florida and around the world.

Now, therefore, be it resolved that I, Frederica S. Wilson, a member of the United States House of Representatives representing the 24th Congressional District of Florida, am honored to recognize the life and legacy of a great man, a great family member, and a great Haitian-American – Daniel Fils-Aimé, Sr.

August 10, 2018

Frederica S. Wilson
Member of Congress

Resolution from the U. S. House of Representatives,
Congresswoman Frederica Wilson honoring
the life and legacy of Daniel Fils-Aimé, Sr.

Proclamation

The City of North Miami, Florida
is pleased to issue this proclamation in honor of

Mr. Daniel Fils-Aime Sr.

WHEREAS, Mr. Daniel Fils-Aime Sr., born in Haiti, May 25th, 1942; and

WHEREAS, Mr. Daniel Fils-Aime, graduated from Lycee Petion High School in Port-au-Prince Haiti, studied Mechanical and Technical Diesel at Avalon Technical School in Montreal Canada and in Brooklyn, New York; and

WHEREAS, Mr. Daniel Fils-Aime, born to parents Fortune MaÇon and Acreus Fils-Aime, succeeded by 2 girls and 3 boys Marcelle, Paula, Daniel Jr., Nonese, Ashley Fils-Aime with wife Eugenie Fils-Aime; and

WHEREAS, Mr. Daniel Fils-Aime was the Founder and Chairman of the Haitian American Historical Society which is the nonprofit organization that built the Haitian Memorial Monument in Savannah Georgia; and

WHEREAS, Mr. Daniel Fils-Aime was the Founder and President of the Miami Minibus Transportation Service Inc., and

WHEREAS, Mr. Daniel Fils-Aime is the Co-Founder of the Haitian American Chamber of Commerce; and

WHEREAS, Mr. Daniel Fils-Aime has become a prolific member of the Haitian Community and abroad through which the Haitian American Historical Society has generated support from numerous public officials at the local, state and federal level where his passion is driven to shed light on the significance of Haitian contributions in American history; and

Now, therefore, in consideration of the foregoing, the Mayor and Council of the City of North Miami do hereby proclaim August 12th, 2018, to be

Dr. Smith Joseph, Mayor

Daniel Fils-Aime Day

in WITNESS WHEREOF, I have hereunto set my hand and caused the seal of the city of North Miami to be affixed this 12th day of August 2018.

Vice Mayor Carol Keys Esq., District 2

Councilman Scott Galvin, District 1

Councilman Phillip Bien-Aime, District 3

Councilman Dr. Alix Desulme, District 4

Larry M. Spring, Jr. City Manager

NORTH MIAMI
F L O R I D A

SEAL

City of North Miami

Proclamation from the City of North Miami
declaring Daniel Fils-Aimé, Sr. Day on August 12, 2018.

Paula Olivier's Doctoral Hooding at Graduation
from United Theological Seminary in December 2012.

Dr. Olivier preaching at a Women's Weekend Retreat
in Florida 2019 with over 1,500 attendees.

Dr. Paula Olivier with bestselling author, speaker, and leadership expert John Maxwell.
Olivier is a certified member of the John Maxwell Team.

Certificate of Commissioning

This Certifies That

Paula Olivier

having given satisfactory evidence of her call to and preparation for the sacred work of the gospel ministry, was commissioned at   Pine Forge, Pennsylvania

on the   4th   *day of*   July   *in the year of our Lord*   2008   *and is duly authorized under the provisions of the Seventh-day Adventist Church to perform all the functions of the ministerial office.*

ISSUED BY THE   *ALLEGHENY EAST*   CONFERENCE OF SEVENTH-DAY ADVENTISTS

President   *Secretary*

Charles L. Cheatham   Henry J. Fordham, III

Dr. Paula Olivier's Commissioning Certificate.
This credential is awarded to pastors by the
Seventh-day Adventist denomination,
generally after earning a Master of Divinity degree
plus a minimum of 5 years of successful ministerial service.

Dr. Paula Olivier
with her husband
Dr. Smith Olivier

About The Author

Dr. Paula (Fils-Aimé) Olivier was born in Brooklyn, NY. She spent the early years of her life in Port-au-Prince, Haiti, and then moved to Miami, FL. She is a graduate of Oakwood University with a B.A. in Ministerial Theology and a minor in Psychology. After Oakwood, she earned a Master of Divinity from Andrews University Theological Seminary and a Doctor of Ministry Degree from United Theological Seminary. She is also a certified John Maxwell Team speaker, trainer and coach.

Pastor Olivier's ministry is both spiritual and innovative. Her preaching ministry has been featured in local and national conferences, radio and television including the Hope Channel and 3ABN. She has spoken across the United States, Canada, Europe, Central America, the Caribbean, Venezuela and Israel.

She is passionate about leadership, motivational speaking and personal growth.

Most people live their lives by default.
I teach them how to live it by design.

Dr. Paula (Fils-Aimé) Olivier

Website: paulaolivier.com

$$48$$
$$+23$$
$$\overline{71}$$
$$29$$
$$\overline{10\ 0}$$

CPSIA information can be obtained
at www.ICGtesting.com
Printed in the USA
LVHW081001300620
659360LV00016B/792

9 781948 877565